A/E/C BUSINESS DEVELOPMENT
The Decade Ahead

SMPS Foundation

Thought Leadership Series Committee

Co-Chairs
Scott W. Braley, FAIA, FRSA
Scott D. Butcher, FSMPS, CPSM

Senior Editor and Proofreader: Jean Leathers, CPSM
Book Cover Design: Nikou McCarra, CPSM
Book Design: Cricket Robertson, CPSM

DEDICATION

The SMPS Foundation dedicates this research effort and book to the hard-working and spirited individuals who buy and sell design and construction services. Their collaboration makes the built environment a better place to live, work, and succeed.

CONTENTS

1 INTRODUCTION

This book is about the buying and selling of design and construction services. Whether you prefer the phrase "design and construction," or the abbreviation "A/E/C" (architecture/engineering/construction), if you buy or sell services in this industry, this book is about and for you.

Our focus is specifically business development. By that we mean the domain of activities and competencies that brings two or more entities—commercial enterprises, government agencies, institutions, or individuals—together in a collaboration focused on a specific project at a specific time.

Business development—often referred to by its nickname "BD"—is about defining needs and making decisions about specific services, identifying and selecting participants, discussing terms and conditions, and concluding the procurement process. In essence, business development is about doing deals and making the proverbial "sale." If you are a buyer or seller of services in this dynamic industry, you are in the right place.

Our caveat is straightforward. This is not a book narrowly focused on traditional approaches, selection processes, cold calls, interviews, negotiations, or other familiar business development practices. You will not find checklists, step-by-step procedures, or faddish tricks or tactics.

What you will find is probing and thoughtful analysis derived from primary research conducted throughout North America during the 2012-2013 timeframe. So, if you are interested in learning more about what business development is like today, and how trends and influences will most likely define and change the process in the decade ahead, read on!

To put these comments and this book itself in perspective, we offer a brief overview of how this effort came about, how the book was created, and how this endeavor furthers the SMPS Foundation's goal of sharing information with those who buy and sell design and construction services. We also offer suggestions for how to get the most out of this book.

What prompted this effort?

This book is a direct realization of SMPS Foundation's essential mission.

A key element of the SMPS Foundation Mission is: "To promote research and education that advances the body of knowledge in the field of professional services marketing."

That fundamental purpose—to advance the body of knowledge in our shared A/E/C industry—was the quintessential spark that ignited the Foundation's research work during the first decade of the 2000s. The SMPS Foundation sponsored a number of subject-specific research efforts, the vast majority of which came to fruition in the form of White Papers. These efforts and their resultant publications became known as the "Thought Leadership Series" (TLS). Secondary research—research that comprised identifying, summarizing, and synthesizing the research work and findings of others—was the principal source of data and information, and a common characteristic of the White Papers. They filled an important need: bringing a wide array of information and data to marketers and business developers in our industry.

In addition to this primary goal within the Foundation Mission, additional goals focused on the value of creating forums and opportunities for SMPS members to more actively engage in helping the A/E/C industry, and SMPS members in particular. Performing research with and by active SMPS members was considered a highly important aspect of this effort.

During the 2011-12 planning year, the SMPS Foundation Board of Trustees identified the need to build upon that solid foundation of research achieved in the TLS, and the opportunity to further advance the body of knowledge. Specifically, the Foundation Trustees wanted to "up the ante" by moving to a conscious and deliberate emphasis on primary research—research efforts that comprise probing for and collecting original data and information directly from the market, then analyzing the information to answer specific questions.

Simultaneously, as the Foundation Trustees moved from secondary to primary research, they also wished to fundamentally change the perspective of the research. The Trustees decided to shift perspective from historical and existing conditions to the future, specifically looking at the future state of business development. The Trustees also expanded the research and intended audience to more evenly balance emphasis on buyers and sellers.

Thus, in 2012, the TLS primary research initiative was born. Having considered a variety of needs and potentials for primary research, the Trustees determined that business development would be the first topic for this concentrated focus. In addition to focus, the Trustees considered how best to share the data and information that resulted from the research.

At the suggestion of two Board Trustees, Scott Braley and Scott Butcher, the Foundation leaders decided to build upon the practice of preparing a series of White Papers to address sub-sets of business development. The Board accepted the recommendation of "the Scotts" to combine the results in a single document that would provide findings to both buyers and sellers of services. The outcome is this book.

Why such a large TLS Committee?

With those general goals in mind, the SMPS Foundation asked Braley and Butcher to lead the initiative. Both were active in the White Paper process, and have strong and accomplished backgrounds and competencies in the design and construction industry.

Braley is an architect and business consultant. His experience is concentrated in design and construction practice, with particular expertise in strategy, leadership, and management. He is a highly-accomplished and recognized "closer-doer" in design, program management, and construction management firms. He served as managing principal in an international design/project management/construction firm that ranked among the Top 40 A/E/C firms headquartered in the United States. There he led efforts from both the buyer's and the seller's perspectives. He is widely published throughout the industry.

Butcher is a seasoned marketer and business developer, with experience marketing architecture, engineering, and construction firms as both prime professional and sub-consultant. A Certified Professional Services Marketer (CPSM), he has served in virtually every marketing and business development function in the design and construction industry. Based upon his accomplishments, he was elevated to Fellow of SMPS in 2011. In addition to these credentials, Butcher also brought a strong background in writing and publishing as the author of a dozen books and numerous articles.

With distinctly different yet highly complementary backgrounds and expertise, Braley and Butcher made a formidable pair to lead the 2012-13 TLS effort.

Braley and Butcher felt strongly that the research should have a comprehensive purview, and that the research and writing effort should be highly collaborative. To accomplish these two goals within the framework of the Foundation's intent, they formed the 2012-13 TLS Committee.

Participating on the TLS Committee to produce this book was a completely voluntary effort. Close to thirty professionals, the majority of whom are CPSMs, volunteered time, resources, and expertise to make this project a reality. More than one-third of the TLS Committee membership is made up of Fellows of SMPS.

By design, the demographics of the TLS Committee can best be summed up in a single phrase: delightfully diverse! The Co-Chairs intentionally sought and assigned volunteers that represented a broad mix of backgrounds that represent the full gamut of design and construction. Geographically, TLS Committee members are located throughout the United States from Maine to California, and from Michigan to Texas.

What is the book's focus and theme?

With an overarching focus on business development, the TLS Committee was charged to explore that singular topic across a broad spectrum of both buyers and sellers of A/E/C services. Beginning with a self-imposed geographic boundary of North America, the TLS Committee formed teams to investigate designated subsets of buyers and sellers.

Concentration on buyer and seller behavior is a key and critical distinction of this research effort. TLS Committee leaders chose not to use traditional, and sometimes eroding, market segment or project type distinctions in the research probes. Rather, they chose to review and analyze the marketplace based on how entities and individuals behave as they lead up to and consummate the "commitment and commercial exchange" that represents the proverbial "sale."

The Co-Chairs' hypothesis was confirmed by the TLS Committee's work: behaviors are consistent—and to a significant degree predictable—across the traditional boundary lines drawn by distinctions such as market, sector, and project type. Few would disagree that a buyer in the private sector has more flexibility in choosing a service provider than his or her counterpart in the public sector.

Just as processes and procedures are relatively more formal and prescriptive in the public sector than private enterprise, so too are the business development behaviors of those individuals who make key decisions and choices.

In addition to the public/private arena, the TLS Committee probed multiple referenced comparisons. They extended the research to test similarities and differences between and among buyer and seller types, services sought and offered, and contracting and project delivery forms.

For example, the TLS Committee examined the highly-focused behaviors of single-service providers versus the entrepreneurial flexibility of multi-discipline providers, as well as those who do both. The list goes on, and we encourage you to study the often-consistent patterns, trends, and root behaviors.

Consequently, you will not find guidance on how to develop business in a particular sector of our industry. Nor is there specific guidance on how to sell services for the design of an airport or a hospital. Similarly, we may disappoint if you are looking for guidance on how to sell construction or related services for an industrial or a defense project.

Rather, you will find research-based guidance on current and future trends about how buyers and sellers behave when they operate within a framework of prescribed procurement regulations and practices. Likewise, you will find insights on how buyers and sellers think about the processes and procedures of business development, regardless of the specific arena or venue in which the deals are made.

The SMPS Foundation's 2012-2013 TLS research project is about what is happing in A/E/C business development now, and what trends are influencing what may happen in the future. The TLS Committee's charge was to begin by addressing the present. This includes what might be seen as as traditional, tried and true approaches to business development, as well as advances and expansion in trends, technology, and the development of cutting-edge approaches to better performance. Better in our positions. Better in our companies. Better in our industry.

As approaches to design standards, technology, communication platforms, marketing, and business development continue to change in our industry, the majority of us still rely on a foundation of fundamentals and know-how already established in our client development routine.

We have our client-approach theories, old reliable scenarios, and steps to winning projects. Yet, we all want to thrive. To excel. Differentiate. Win. That's what this book is about.

How did this book come together?

Comprised of multiple members, each research/writing team concentrated on a predetermined type of buyer or seller. With primary research as the criterion, each team relied most heavily on direct or virtual face-to-face interviews. In all cases, contacts focused on key decision-makers and those in positions of power to influence the procedural and outcome decisions surrounding the business development process that leads to the ultimate sale.

More than 100 one-on-one interviews were completed across the full spectrum of buyers and sellers. These were supplemented by numerous data and information sourcing activities, such as monitoring client and A/E/C provider panels at which the focus topics were discussed and debated.

To ensure consistency across the array of those interviewed, a set of core baseline questions were asked in all interviews. (See Chapter 13 – Baseline Research Questions). In all cases, the TLS Committee researchers and interviewers began with these questions. Predictably and by design these queries led to many other topics and discussions.

In each case, the teams consolidated the data and information gathered, then analyzed it for those influences that were most powerful, and those behaviors that were most consistent. The research data was then codified and organized to paint a clear picture of how buyers and sellers think and behave now, and how they are being influenced to think and behave in the decade ahead.

The initial research and writing tasks were organized by segmenting the diverse design and construction marketplace based on the highly distinct characteristics of buyers and sellers.

Buyers were cataloged by essential distinctions that were most likely to influence behavior, such as: public versus private arenas, for-profit versus not-for-profit, and formal/procedural versus informal/entrepreneurial.

Sellers were segmented based on behavior influences, such as: single- versus multiple-service providers, designers versus builders, and primes versus sub-consultants.

Research and writer teams, typically made up of two or three individuals, probed deeply into each of these focused behavioral and characteristic segments. In each case, the primary research team documented its findings in the form of a draft chapter for this book.

Subsequently, a large team of analysts and writers further analyzed the data—verifying and testing the initial findings, as well as discerning patterns and trends of behavior.

Finally, a small group of writers and editors made one last pass through the work to add a measure of consistency among the various findings, patterns, and trends, while preserving the individual voice and tone of the original authors' work.

How can you get the most out of this book?

The research results presented in this book are structured in two parts: Part 1 – Sellers of A/E/C Services, and Part 2 – Buyers of A/E/C Services. In each case, chapters focus on a specific sub-set of the primary category—

those buyers or sellers who are aligned around and defined by a consistent set of characteristics and resultant behaviors.

We suggest you begin by focusing on those buyers or sellers whose characteristics are most familiar to your work, or with whom you identify most at the individual or enterprise level.

The TLS Committee researchers and analysts have summarized key ideas and conclusions at the end of each chapter. In addition, summaries of findings and forecasts are provided for sellers at the end of Part 1, and for buyers at the end of Part 2.

In our view, the quick study reader or skimmer—those wanting only the executive summary version of this research—will be well served to go right to these summaries at the end of each chapter and the major parts of the book, before returning to read the book from cover to cover. Those looking for more detail and background on the interdependent and evolving subtleties and nuances of future success will want to begin with the first chapter and move sequentially through both the seller and buyer sections.

We wish you well as you enjoy and use this book. Moreover, we extend our best to you as you succeed in the decade ahead! We are grateful for the opportunity to play a part in supporting your success.

PART 1 – SELLERS OF A/E/C SERVICES

2 SHARP SHOOTERS
Single-discipline Prime

Researchers/Authors: Colleen Kucera, CPSM; Melissa Lutz, FSMPS, CPSM; Lori Miller, CPSM, ExecCoach

Analysts/Editors: Janet E. Brooks, CPSM; Katie van der Sleesen

Definition

This chapter focuses on single-discipline design and planning firms of varying sizes and service types that typically conduct business development as the primary contact with an owner or client. The business development function is likely to be the responsibility of principals and projects managers following the seller-doer model, and may or may not be supported by marketing and business development staff. These firms may also form teams with other consultants for their marketing and business development approach to specific projects or clients.

Research Design

The research approach entailed a series of qualitative, primary interviews held in person and over the telephone. The firms and individuals selected for interview have proven themselves in their respective industries as leaders and strategists.

What are your most effective current strategies and approaches to business development?

The general consensus among firms interviewed regarding the most effective strategy to employ is to focus on keeping clients happy. The goal is to build a long-term relationship with the client, and this was considered to be the most important step in business development. A firm that does good work for their client hopes to continue to be hired by them, and hopes it will generate other business through referrals received from those clients.

One comment made by Rich DeYoung, Principal of WTW Architects, brings the element of personal chemistry and its impact on successful business development strategies into focus. He noted that, "We're in a period of quickly shifting sands right now and I feel that personal chemistry is a big part of the final decision-making process for clients and potential clients. We have found that there are many more clients demanding concepts and ideas, so they make a decision based on a concept, rather than process. But, I think, even with concepts and ideas–personal chemistry still trumps it all. The client has to feel like they want to work with you and that you're going to have their back."

A component of building long-term client relationships is the role that staff retention plays. Staff turnover was considered by the interviewees to be viewed negatively by clients. The concern raised was that when a firm shows a lot of turnover during the management of a project or firm overall, the client might feel uneasy and look for a firm that is able to demonstrate more stability by being able to sustain their staff without a lot of change. As a result, considerable importance was placed on communicating to the client and the marketplace about their staff retention track record.

Clients shortlist a specific team from a proposal and they expect to see those individuals at the interview. After selection, the interview team is also the team that the client assumes they will be working with throughout the project. When those team members change, trust can deteriorate.

Communicating with the client as soon as changes are necessary is always best. Interviewees felt that this would enhance the level of comfort that clients have in the firm, as well as feel assured that the people currently working with them would continue to maintain the relationship for years to come. Clients do not like the element of surprise from their chosen team.

A related theme was the impact of staff turnover—when it does happen—on the client relationship. Of equal importance are the actions a firm takes to retain the client when a project manager or team leader moves to another company or retires. It was considered essential for firms to communicate this to the client and have a plan in place to assure the client that their needs would be met and that they should see no difference in the level of service the firm is providing.

Another strategy being implemented by the firms interviewed focuses on broadening staff understanding of the tools and techniques of business development. This is a strategy that the interviewees indicate that they plan to continue to place an emphasis on for everyone in their firms, not just principals and project managers.

Jay Kuhn of Process Plus stated, "We have to train our technical people to think of sales in the back of their minds when meeting with clients. You have to think about who people know, and you have to follow them when they move from one position to the next and one company to the next."

The importance of hiring designated marketing/business development staff was another strategy discussed. Most of the firms currently have full-time marketing/business development staff, and those that did not, have their principals assuming all the responsibility for bringing in work. For these firms, the common theme is that the principals are then stretched in many different directions and their focus is taken away from running their business and completing projects for their clients. The firms who do not have designated staff who are responsible for business development have put plans in place to hire a full-time person for this function in the future.

How have you changed your strategies and approaches to business development in recent years?

Many of the firms interviewed mentioned that strategies had to be changed in order to keep up with the competition. Competition has grown across the country. One of the key issues that single-discipline firms have been facing is that larger, multi-service firms are pursuing smaller projects that were not part of their business development plans in the past. This is forcing smaller and mid-size firms to ramp up their business development and marketing activities.

One key approach being used by firms is to become more client focused rather than project focused. "Midstate Mechanical has become more focused on project pursuits at an earlier point in the project. Clients are demanding more of an integrated delivery approach, which brings us into the pursuit process at a much earlier phase," said Lisa McFate, Marketing Manager at Midstate Mechanical.

"Understanding our clients, as well as our client's client, is much more important these days than understanding one specific project," said Lisa Bentley at McCarthy Nordburg. To do this, they spend more time listening to their clients.

Additionally, clients are becoming extremely sophisticated and educated. Most know about a firm's services and offerings before they have a project. It is important for firms to understand the priorities that the client has at the proposal stage so that the proposal and work focus on exceeding their needs and expectations.

A long-term relationship is seen to serve firms much more than targeting one specific project at a time. With the focus on long-term relationships, several firms mentioned that gaining knowledge of the inner workings of their clients' businesses was a key business development strategy. In recent years, Champlin Architecture has been focused on the culture of their individual clients. Now, repeat clients form 85 percent of their business. For another design firm interviewed, over 98 percent of their projects last year were for repeat clients. Again, it was noted that staff changes directly relate to client relationship changes. If the goal for firm success is to build and maintain relationships, then it is important to have a plan in place to nurture the client relationship so that client does not follow a project manager that leaves.

One large recent industry change is the departure from having just a few individuals responsible for all of the business development efforts. As mentioned earlier, more firms are emphasizing that business development—though directed from top management—is the focus of everyone in the firm.

Developing and strengthening alliances is another approach recently being taken in our industry. Alliances allow firms to expand their service offerings, as well as benefit from each other's client networks. It positions firms to be introduced to clients who may have relationships with their alliance partners at an earlier stage in a project's process than they might otherwise be able to achieve. Firms are then positioned to assist the client with initial project issues, allowing them to establish a relationship with the client, which hopefully leads to winning more work from the client.

Some of the interviewees whose firms seek to develop business with architecture firms mentioned that their focus is on strengthening their alliances with both architecture firms and general contracting firms in order to get more of the work up front. Positioning your firm with another service firm is accomplished when trust is built and you are so entwined with their business that you become their preferred firm for the services you provide.

Fee-driven selection was a rising concern for all of the firms interviewed. A few interviewees mentioned the notion that their clients were more attracted to low cost rather than value. The approach mentioned was that professional services firms needed to sell their value proposition to the client. To do this, it was seen to be important for firms to position themselves with high value services to avoid continually having their services viewed as a commodity. A key point is to find creative ways for strategic positioning.

One approach taken by Midstate Mechanical was to expand their capabilities. They are currently in the process of merging three companies under one roof. This has required a rebranding effort, market positioning, business development, information technology implementation, and review and consolidation of all business functions.

Lisa McFate, Marketing Manager with Midstate Mechanical, said, "Each company brings its own set of services. These services create a continuum of expertise and assistance that our clients can access at any point in the life of their building. And because each service is related to the others, the entire cycle is strengthened with every project."

Another approach is being able to change, adapt, and stay relevant in the marketplace. Skip Allen with McCarthy Nordburg sums it up: "Being a twenty-six-year-old firm, we have to counterbalance the stability and longevity of the firm while still being able to change, adapt, and be fresh with today's ever-changing market."

For their work, they need to understand the current multi-generational workforce and how this affects their design strategies. They have to be able to adapt and sell this flexibility to their clients. He also stated that they need to promote their interior design services to clients as a way of attracting and retaining the best workforce.

What changes do you plan to make in the future regarding either strategy or business approach to business development?

Although most firms are doing more with less, all are finding the time to devote to business development and marketing strategy. The firms interviewed already invest in marketing and business developments efforts and plan to continue to do so.

Almost every firm interviewed mentioned that they would need to shift their mindset from simply providing services to running a knowledge-based practice. Being seen as an expert is a way to stand out from the competition and allow firms to differentiate themselves. "The dog and pony show is going away along with the old wine and dine with clients. Business development has become more and more based on an educational process with our clients," said Sue Sylvester with Midstate Mechanical.

Today, professional services firms need to be flexible as change is rapid within the A/E/C industry. They will need to continue to determine ways to provide innovative solutions to their client's needs in order to grow. The need for firms to provide additional services to meet these client needs may open the door for creative partnering with other firms who can complement their services offerings. Many firms are identifying their alliance partners for particular service niches early on and forming relationships to be prepared when an opportunity arises.

"Recently, a client needed a deeper area of expertise than what we offer. We called on an alliance partner who had five to ten people with this type of in-depth knowledge and presented them as our process piping partner. This works both ways as we can offer complementary services. Our alliance partners also call us to help meet their clients' needs, as well," said Jay Kuhn at Process Plus.

Other firms also mentioned forming strategic alliances with firms around the country as a lead generator for a particular service offering.

Richard DeYoung, Principal with WTW Architects, said, "They bring us onto the team for our expertise in a particular building type. We pursue a specific project together and win it. Then, when the next opportunity presents itself, they bring us in again and again. This kind of strategic alliance has grown more than anything in the last five to ten years."

All agreed that focus on the client would never go out of fashion. The business model of the successful A/E/C firm will be centered on serving the client's needs. If the client wants a service, then they need a firm to provide that service in an exceptional manner. Partnering was mentioned as a component of project delivery plans, and several firms mentioned partnering as an approach to project management.

"It's important that our clients connect the firm and its work to our staff that provide the service to them," said Gregory Calabria, President of Dodson Engineering. "To me, the project is only as successful as the people doing it and the outcome ties directly to business development and our ability to maintain repeat clients."

Another common thread was the emphasis on team building to strengthen the core employees at firms. Each firm has weathered the economic shift over the last few years. They are now in a position to grow and provide effective, creative solutions as the economy continues to grow stronger. Each firm has been working to train their project managers to take on business development mindsets and responsibilities.

Jay Kuhn at Process Plus said, "The seminar we really need to develop is one which trains our technical people on how to answer questions—not to just answer yes or no—but to offer technical and specific solutions to their challenges. Along with this is training them to ask the right questions. We have to teach our technical people how to ask for the next job. We tell them not to be scared to death. We want them to ask about the client's capital budget and to ask them where their pains are and how we can help. The focus of our training is how to be a salesperson for the firm without being a car salesperson."

As you look forward to the next ten years, what trends and considerations will most influence how you conduct business development to offer design services?

It is important that firms stick to their marketing plans and be proactive, rather than reactive in spite of unstable market conditions.

Identifying future trends and thinking strategically was also a point of discussion. "It is crucial to our practice to stay ahead of the game. This allows us to be the preferred provider of architectural services to our clients and will keep them coming back to us for advice on critical issues regarding their space," said Joan Wurtenberger, Senior Principal with Champlin

Architecture. Being an industry thought leader to their clients and partners is becoming more important.

Selecting a process that is good for your firm, based on what has and hasn't worked, is also seen to be important. "Everybody's changing their process. There's this dynamic going on in the industry. I know it will be different and we have to pay attention so we can respond and be successful," said Richard DeYoung, Principal with WTW Architects.

The firms interviewed all discussed a continued emphasis on business development as a key element in their business strategy. Many firms mentioned reconnecting with existing clients with whom they have done successful projects in the past. This confirms a general rule of thumb that it takes more time and marketing dollars to develop a new relationship than to nurture an existing one. One firm operating a branch office is evaluating the potential of hiring an employee to focus solely on business development and marketing when the firm principals would typically have done this. Targeting and researching prospective clients is also expected to gain in importance.

Another area of concern was the discussion of fees and the impact during the selection process. It seems that owners/clients are placing additional emphasis on the level of fees for fee-based services. Most firms would like to believe that the level of experience is tied directly to the selection of firms. However, there are also a great number of professional services firms and some of them are willing to cut their fees to win the work and build their backlog.

During the latest recession, there was an identifiable trend of clients basing their selection on low cost, rather than depth of experience or proven abilities. To address this, the interviewees felt that firms in this industry must offer sophisticated services at a fair cost to minimize being viewed as a commodity by their clients. As the world is evolving with new technologies and processes by which to design projects, there is a strong feeling that firms must stay ahead of the trends. These trends all come with a newly needed skillset and fees will have to be adjusted over time as the industry perfects these skills.

Political influence is also becoming a point of contention for several of the firms interviewed. Knowing about the political shifts and trends for funding is important when pursuing particular niches such as biomedical, health care, education, and transportation. It is becoming more important to support clients in identifying funding avenues for their projects.

The impact and influence of social media on the way firms promote themselves and communicate in the market will continue to grow. When developing marketing plans, it will be important to place a value on social media and consider it when positioning the firm.

17

As Michael Miller, Principal of Barber Hoffman said, "You have to be visible, especially in today's techno-world. I used to talk with clients more over the telephone. Today social media outlets are bridges that can bring you closer to your clients and partners. We need to identify other ways to be visible with our clients and potential clients."

The use of video interviews and testimonials is becoming much more prevalent in promotional efforts and will need to be considered by firms.

Another area that firms are expected to include in their marketing mix is the development of blogs as a way to connect with clients. The focus of all these efforts will be on getting a firm's credentials in front of the people and companies that have been targeted and researched carefully. It will be increasingly important that firms provide thoughtful information to their clients in the medium that they are comfortable with using as an information source.

"We need to be noticed by our clients," said Michael Miller of Barber Hoffman. "One of the things I want to implement over the next few years is mandating that my junior leaders develop lunch and learn seminars and meet with their client contacts to discuss some aspect of structural design. In other words, face time is still a very important part of our business."

So, with this thought, which one thing will you focus on in the coming years?

- Building and strengthening personal relationships with clients and partners.
- Retaining great personnel.
- Improving the ability to articulate firm and professional service value propositions.
- Enhancing reputation and visibility within the industry and with clients.

3 COLLABORATORS
Sub-consultants and Specialty Consultants

Researchers/Authors: Scott D. Butcher, FSMPS, CPSM; Emily Crandall, CPSM; Diana Soldano, FSMPS, CPSM

Analyst/Editor: Kim Icenhower, FSMPS, CPSM

Definition

This chapter addresses sub-consultants and specialty consultants—firms that perform at least 50 percent of their work as a consultant to an architect, engineer, or contractor, and do not hold a contract directly with the owner.

Research Design

A series of qualitative interviews were conducted with senior and executive staff of A/E firms and specialty consultants that average at least 50 percent of their annual revenue coming as a sub-consultant to an architect, engineer, contractor, or related firm. The interviews were held in-person, over the telephone, and via electronic means. Information obtained during a panel discussion hosted by the SMPS Philadelphia Chapter entitled, "The Art and Science of Business Development," was also incorporated into the research. At the 2012 Build Business, SMPS National Conference, a roundtable discussion was held with business developers from specialty and sub-consultants, and elements of those conversations are also included.

What are your most effective current strategies and approaches to business development?

The "Great Recession" had a major impact on the design and construction industry, forcing companies to re-evaluate their business development approaches. Many of these companies do not have dedicated business development staff, relying on principals and project managers to serve as seller-doers, in some cases supported by dedicated marketing staff.

At the top of many executives' minds right now is providing a high level of service to existing clients, since current clients comprise the bulk of most firms' revenues.

Steve P. Osborn, PE, SE, FSMPS, CPSM, Principal/President of Indiana-based CE Solutions, Inc. Structural Engineers, noted that, "A mantra around our office is 'relationships first, opportunities second.' We focus on building and nurturing relationships at all levels, through a variety of networking and communications activities. When you help others, others help you, and you become advocates for one another."

Project managers are a key component for most firms' business development strategies, with project managers often tasked with maintaining relationships with their clients after project completion. Called "Client Managers" or "Account Managers," these individuals are responsible for mining their accounts and leveraging existing relationships to expand their service offerings to clients, finding new opportunities at other client locations, and keeping the competition away by "taking projects of the street" before they are even announced.

Thomas Townes, AIA, FSMPS, CPSM, Director of Business Development for Van Note–Harvey Associates, PC, a New Jersey-based civil engineering firm, has a unique perspective. He formerly owned his own architectural practice, Focus Architecture, so he pursued work as a prime professional. He found that his true passion was business development, not architecture, so he joined a firm that does half of its work as a sub-consultant to other A/E/C firms.

> "Business development is all about relationship building, and that's not going to change," said Thomas Townes. "When you're in a down economy, one thing that you cannot afford to do is forget the ones who got you where you are."

Townes believes that a lot of opportunities are lost by not maintaining relationships with past clients, who may not have any work for a few years, but often do have more work at a later date. Project managers who are too focused on serving other relationships, or business developers who are too engrossed in developing new accounts, ignore a great existing connection and miss out on future opportunities.

For companies that do have dedicated business development staff, those individuals' primary focus is often finding new clients.

Several interviewees noted that they use old-fashioned direct mail: letters, postcards, or anything else sent via the U.S. Postal Service. While many firms are using various electronic marketing approaches for sales prospecting, the significant decline in direct mail has given some firms an opportunity to break through the clutter and stand out—especially compared to the deluge of emails most people receive on a daily basis.

Getting involved with client associations is a primary strategy for McClave Engineering, an eighteen-person consulting engineering firm located in Port Jefferson, New York. The firm does not have any staff dedicated only to business development, and those involved with the business development process are engineers. Pat McClave, Vice President, believes that association involvement alone is not enough, and that getting involved at the committee level is essential.

Schaefer, a consulting structural engineering firm, targets architects and contractors, as well as owners. They focus on building their professional networks through organizations where A/E/C firms or owners congregate, including SMPS, local chambers of commerce, Builders Exchange of Ohio, Urban Land Institute, U.S. Green Building Council, and American Institute of Architects, among others.

According to Ryan M. Konst, PE, Managing Director of their Columbus, Ohio office, "We leverage these relationships into project opportunities, and eventually projects."

Deborah Raw, CPSM, Marketing Director for TCT Cost Consultants LLC, believes that, "The key to success at these events is pre-event planning and immediate follow-up after the event." TCT also uses pre-proposal conferences as a rich environment where they find their targeted audience all in one room at the same time.

The value of client associations is that they offer a way to meet prospective clients on neutral territory. Through working at the committee level, close relationships can be forged, with the representative from the A/E/C firm increasingly being viewed as a friend or supporter of the organization. According to Terry Kilbourne, President of TEC Inc. Engineering & Design in Eastlake, Ohio, his business developer also uses professional organizations to gain valuable intelligence like trends or forthcoming legislation that he can share with both existing and prospective clients. In the process, he is able to position himself, and his company, as a valuable resource. Kilbourne believes that involvement in professional organizations with your friends and competitors is important, but being active in client associations is critical.

Acoustics Dimensions, a technology and acoustic specialty consultant with offices in three states and the United Kingdom, takes a relationship-centric approach to new business development. They know that 85 percent of their annual volume comes from existing clients, so they focus their new business efforts on leveraging that existing network. Cathy Hutchison, LEED AP, Vice President and Director of Marketing for the company's Dallas office, sums it up this way: "Who knows who knows who?"

They are proactive about getting referrals from their existing clients. Using a heavy research component, they identify their prospects, why it makes sense to pursue them, and how they can help them. Then they map out the degrees of separation between them and the prospect, and use their client network to make introductions to get them one step closer to the person they are trying to meet.

How effective are your current strategies and approaches to business development, and do you see them changing in the future?

Tried and true business development strategies aren't necessarily as effective as they used to be. Everyone agrees that face-to-face contact is absolutely critical to developing relationships, and this will not change in the future. But the way to get those meetings has changed, and in the current economic climate it is increasingly more difficult to gain an audience with decision makers.

While some firms still attempt cold calling, their results have declined in recent years. One example is a business developer who made several hundred prospecting calls, but only had a half-dozen people actually answer the phone. Voice mail and caller identification is omnipresent, and the odds of a return call are exceptionally low. According to some publishing metrics, it often takes ten attempts and voice mails before making contact with a prospect. Most people give up after the first or second call, so when using this approach, tenacity is critical.

Many firms have broadened their sales efforts to more market segments in the belief that while some markets may not be spending, others will be. However, they also report that the business development efforts get stretched extremely thin and the firm tends to be viewed more as a generalist and not a niche consultant, so they are battling perceptions.

Interestingly, firms are moving in different directions. Some cast a wider net while others focus only on the highest value opportunities and clients. Geographic expansion was mentioned by several interviewees as a newer business development strategy, although the results have been mixed as the firms are finding it difficult to be an unknown player in a new geographic market, competing against the established firms with a breadth and depth of relationships.

Another change in business development is the introduction of Public Private Partnerships, which are becoming standard in many market sectors, as is an increase in design/build projects. Firms need to address these elements in their business model and adjust their strategies accordingly.

The phrase "next year" was mentioned a lot by interviewees. Next year our markets will improve. Next year we'll be able to hire a full-time business developer. Next year we'll change our marketing approach. Next year we are going to develop a Business Development Strategy Plan.

Many firms seem to be hunkered down, focused on existing relationships while facing a very difficult task in developing new relationships because of increased competition and a difficult economy.

Terry Kilbourne believes that there are four major drivers that impact business development: "The economy has changed, competition has changed, fees have become tighter, and deadlines are shorter."

Furthermore, Kilbourne has noticed a change in loyalties in the A/E community during his forty years in the profession. "Years ago clients were very loyal. You started with them, and if you did a good job, then you were in good shape and fees didn't matter. This has changed dramatically now, and the architectural community does not always value engineering services to the level they should. They become a necessary evil," said Kilbourne. As evidence of this, he points to a recent hour-long client interview, with only seven minutes for the mechanical, electrical, and plumbing (MEP) team to make their case.

Schaefer has recently reorganized the way they approach business development. They have dedicated team members including a director, managers, and coordinators, but these are engineers with a certain percentage of their time dedicated to business development. The firm has found greater success with technical staff handling the sales efforts as opposed to non-technical business developers.

According to Ryan Konst, "The old way was not working. There was no information sharing or accountability between offices and teams. With the addition of a marketing manager in the last year, there are now more resources for supporting business development efforts. This position has also helped with the strategy and laser focus."

One of the most effective business development strategies embraced by Acoustic Dimensions has been education. "All of our offices have an educational wing," said Cathy Hutchison. "We must bring value to a person's time, so there has to be tangible value to every conversation. It can't be just a sales thing, or we'd come across as a used car salesman."

This educational approach varies by office and seller-doer. Some team members develop new business by going out and presenting, armed with AIA Learning Units. They target architectural practices, professional associations, or anywhere else that they can reach an audience. Other seller-doers focus on education in one-on-one conversations, making themselves available for day-long brainstorming sessions to help architectural clients or prospects win the work they are pursuing.

"We really take time to tailor what we are doing to the audience, whether it's one-on-one, a lunch-and-learn with fifteen people, or a presentation at an industry conference," said Hutchison.

Electronic marketing efforts have proven effective to an executive with a mid-Atlantic engineering firm. "This past year we transitioned from a static, irregularly updated website to one hosted on a blogging platform, in this case WordPress. We have been blogging and expanding our social media outreach, more so by key employees, as opposed to the company. As a result we've seen a significant traffic increase to our website, and more than $600,000 in revenue this year as a result of prospects finding us online, and contacting us. Plus, there are even more opportunities in the pipeline, so it has become a great lead source. We definitely plan to not only continue what we are doing, but ramp it up to provide even more content and expand our outreach."

How have you changed your strategies and approaches to business development in recent years, and do you see these changes as short term or permanent?

Technical staff involvement in the business development process has been increasing in recent years, and this change is viewed as permanent by many, due both to the need to reduce overhead expenses for A/E firms, as well as client drivers. According to the vice president of a mid-sized MEP firm headquartered in Pennsylvania, "Our project managers and vice presidents are now more involved with the business development process than they used to be, and this is a permanent change for our firm."

While most firms have historically had Business Plans and Marketing Plans, a new trend is emerging: the Business Development Plan. Andrew Weinberg, CPSM of WorkingBuildings, a building commissioning firm based in Atlanta, Georgia, said, "We are going to develop a Business Development Strategy Plan, which would include client type, regions, etc. This would be a permanent change."

Thomas Townes believes that the seller-doer model is the future, even though he jokes that it would make his job unnecessary. "More emphasis needs to be made on coaching key individuals to become business developers."

Townes noted that not every technical person has the skills to do business development, but the top performers need to elevate their skills in this area, because ten or twelve seller-doers can have a far greater reach than a single, dedicated business developer. In the short-term, he doesn't see an increase in business development hiring within the design and construction industry, but expects a level field for a few years. Longer-term, however, Townes believes that as owners become more sophisticated, there will be fewer dedicated sellers in favor of the more technical seller-doers.

Conversely, though, some firms are recognizing the value of dedicated marketing staff, particularly if they can partially pay for their position. According to Steven Osborn, the biggest change at CE Solutions was bringing a full-time marketing director to the firm in 2009, which is a permanent change.

> "In addition to directing and managing the marketing function, our marketing director is also involved with business development efforts, and offers marketing communications consulting to our clients, which provides an additional revenue stream for the firm," said Steven Osborn at CE Solutions.

Terry Kilbourne echoes the importance of having dedicated staff. "We hired our first business development person four years ago in the throes of the economic downturn. Now I can't imagine not having someone in the role." Kilbourne owns Tec Inc. Engineering & Design with two partners. All are involved with business development; however, their participation level has lessened since the full-time business developer was hired. Based upon the results of the position, this is a permanent change.

One of the interviewees noted that there is definitely a role for a non-technical business developer at his company; however, there are two drawbacks. First, dedicated salespeople tend to view the world with rose-colored glasses, so the next project or big opportunity is always just around the corner. Second, there is a potential negative perspective that prospective clients may have, viewing a salesperson as someone trying to get their business, rather than as a liaison to technical professionals.

So what role can that person play? According to the executive, the dedicated business developer can be a bird-dog, maintain regular contact, share information internally and externally, and help technical staff be more effective in their business development roles.

Specialty and sub-consulting firms are also looking toward social media as a way to drive their message. Here sub-consulting firms have an advantage when compared to A/E/C firms that serve as prime professionals. The prime firms often have difficulty connecting directly with owners via social networking sites like LinkedIn. However, A/E/C firms are increasingly present on these sites, creating an opportunity for consultants to reach out and connect with them.

According to the 2012 SMPS Technology Survey, 78 percent of respondents indicated that their firms use LinkedIn, with 53 percent using Facebook, and 46 percent using Twitter. This creates a great opportunity for sub-consulting firms to develop networks by connecting on LinkedIn, following Tweets, and joining groups where target clients are members.

"We have adopted social media as a communication tool and plan to ramp it up even more in the future," said Steven Osborn. "This is a permanent change, as we see social media as another way to communicate. However, our approach to it will evolve as social media evolves."

"We're not using social media the way we can, and the way we should," said Thomas Townes. He has changed the way he approaches business development by integrating LinkedIn as a major tool. Early in his career, Townes knew a salesperson who regularly sent him clippings from newspapers and magazines—articles that the salesperson thought might be of interest. Today, Townes employs this approach but via LinkedIn. He will even go as far as to scan an article with his smartphone, save it as a PDF, upload it to his LinkedIn account, and send it out to his connections that could benefit from the information—all while enjoying his morning coffee at the local coffee shop.

"It's a soft approach. It's getting them information. It's not pressing or badgering them. You can annoy people! A soft approach to maintaining contact is through social media, if you're careful, and if you can use LinkedIn to that advantage," said Townes. This is a permanent change for Townes, and the next step is to get his company to become more involved with social media.

Hiara Guevara-Delgado, Director of CSM Engineering, PC, a D/M/WBE engineering and construction inspection firm based in Uniondale, NY, echoes that sentiment. Guevara-Delgado, whose firm's repeat business is about 90 percent annually, said, "We have to use more social media marketing to give the firm exposure. These changes would be permanent for the next ten years."

Some companies that have previously shied away from community organizations have recently become engaged in an attempt to strengthen their local efforts and meet new prospects.

One of the most pronounced changes identified by interviewees is a shake-up in their clients. Because of the heated competition and changing loyalties, sub-consultants and specialty consultants are increasingly looking to become prime professionals themselves. And if the end-goal is not necessarily to become the prime, these firms find great value in developing relationships with owners and end-users because it ultimately creates more opportunities. Owners may recommend them—or even require their inclusion on teams—to A/E/C primes proposing for work.

Furthermore, if a sub-consultant has forged a positive relationship with an owner, then a prime A/E/C firm may be more interested in collaborating with the sub-consultant because of that relationship. Ultimately this may help to position the team more favorably in the eyes of the owner.

Ryan Konst believes this will be a permanent change: "At the end of the day, the owner always makes the final decision of what team to hire and having a relationship with them will make the firm more appealing, even if their contract is directly with the architect."

Tec Inc. has taken this philosophy and made it part of their corporate culture. Their recently tweaked mission and vision statements claim they "aspire to be the engineering and design partner that clients insist upon."

Pat McClave echoes this belief. "We are focusing on owners, rather than the A/E/C community because the owners recommend consultants. Recommendations hold a lot of weight."

At the 2012 Build Business research session, participants agreed that sub-consultants need to evolve from just selling to architects, engineers, or contractors, and develop a multi-channel business development model that also includes the owners. By speaking the owner's language, and becoming their advocate, the sub-consultants can make themselves more valuable team members to the primes chasing the work. This approach also helps avoid the commodity trap.

Acoustic Dimensions has found themselves increasingly reacting to the need for speed. "We have had to become extremely fast! When I started here sixteen years ago, we often had two weeks to prepare a proposal. Now we frequently have twenty-four hours, or less," said Cathy Hutchison. As a result, the company culture is geared toward quick response, whether it is turning around a proposal in less than a day, or providing detailed project budgets to help their clients make informed decisions in a short timeframe. "High quality, fast turn-around has become the cultural norm at Acoustic Dimensions." Hutchison identifies three components to this: 1) technology, 2) processes, 3) people.

What changes do you plan to make as you approach business development during the next ten years, and do you think these will be temporary or permanent changes?

"Image is Everything" used to be the tagline for Canon, a manufacturer of cameras. The saying holds true for many A/E/C sub-consultants, too. Several interviewees indicated that focusing on their image is an important component of their business development efforts moving forward.

> "We are rebranding our company so that the image we portray is consistent with both external perceptions and our internal aspirations. We also plan to overhaul our website," said Steve Osborne.

Schaefer recently completed a major rebranding initiative, including changing the company name from Steven Schaefer Associates.

Other firms are looking to diversify. At Tec Inc., related services like arc flash consulting, technology design, and lighting design have bolstered their more traditional MEP offerings. In fact, lighting design has become a specialty, and a key differentiator from other MEP firms. However, Tec Inc. moved beyond just ramping up their marketing for the service. They launched a new company—Tec Studio—to provide lighting design and technology. It is a WBE and EDGE (Encouraging Diversity, Growth, and Equity) certified firm, which Kilbourne believes will open many new doors previously closed to them.

CE Solutions and Schaefer believe that changes in technology will drive their business over the next decade. Both firms are planning to move forward with Customer Relationship Management (CRM) systems. In the short-term, Schaefer is moving forward with an implementation of the Cosential CRM product.

Said Ryan Konst: "Many consultants have not made this jump yet, but there is a huge value in having all business development information and history in one easy-to-access database." Eventually he hopes that this information will assist the marketing department with proposals and qualifications submissions.

Schaefer will also increasingly rely on social media as part of their marketing mix. They will be launching a new social media-friendly website which Konst believes will help to expand their reach.

Acoustic Dimensions utilizes the Observe, Orient, Decide, Act (OODA) loop to stay in tune with the changes around them. The OODA loop moves decision-making through a cycle-driven process, ensuring that they are able to quickly react to market changes.

Cathy Hutchison said, "There are three drivers in a continual state of flux: economic, cultural, and technology." About their approach she commented, "It's like building the bridge as we walk on it." Recently that has meant that they needed to diversify their target markets as the company's three primary markets changed. The result was a retooling of offerings to serve the new markets.

As you look toward the next decade, what trends and considerations will most influence how you conduct business development to offer design and construction services?

When asked about the industry changes that will impact their firms over the next decade, responses were varied.

Acoustic Dimensions aims to ensure their relevance by embracing Revit software, obtaining a high percentage of staff with the LEED AP designation (currently at 70 percent), and focusing on being an early collaborative member on every project and professional services team in which they are involved.

According to Cathy Hutchison, "The next ten years will be about three things: building information modeling, sustainability, and integrated project delivery."

The vice president of a mid-sized MEP engineering firm noted that there are four critical questions that must be answered:

- Who will be making the selection for professional services?
- How will professional services be offered?
- What are the expected services from professional providers?
- Will the client require or expect licensed staff to call on them as part of the business development process?

Steve Osborn believes that creativity will be the key: "In an ever-increasing competitive landscape, clients are looking for consultants that can bring them creative ideas and help do their jobs more effectively. If a client sees all firms as equal, the decision of which firm to use becomes price-driven. It's up to all of us to learn as much as we can about the clients we serve and want to serve and what opportunities exist to help them."

Osborn sees the roles of sub-consultants changing in the coming years: "These opportunities might not fit the traditional roles we have played in the past, so we have to be flexible and creative in our approaches and ask ourselves what we can do to help our clients achieve their goals."

CSM Engineering believes that with the increased competition in the industry, their firm needs to be up-to-date on technology in order to compete in the future. Hiara Guevara-Delgado said, "Doing business as usual is no longer accepted."

Project delivery methods have changed, and the impact on specialty firms and sub-consultants was noted by several interviewees. Increased marketing to design-builders and construction managers is a natural reaction for this segment of the A/E/C industry, particularly with 50 percent of all construction projects going the design-build route, and as much as 80 percent of projects by some owners—the Department of Defense, for example—going design-build.

McClave Engineering has felt an impact from this trend, and Pat McClave believes that, "Owners want a set fee and want to have the project team work together from the beginning."

In the State of Ohio, the government is changing its delivery model, and moving toward construction management at-risk and design-build as its contracting methods. Terry Kilbourne said, "With this change in delivery models there needs to be an effort to develop relationships with construction managers and contractors now, so there's a need to move from strictly dealing with architects to the construction management and contractor side of the business."

Evidence-based design came up in several conversations. Though it impacts firms primarily in the health care industry right now, there is a belief that "proof of concept" is going to spread across all markets. Design and consulting firms will have to elevate their collection of lessons learned from projects, and also assemble their own research, to inform business development efforts and position themselves as thought leaders in their primary market segments.

"Tit-for-tat" was a trend that several participants mentioned. In order to gain business from new companies, or even to maintain existing relationships, prime professionals are increasingly expecting sub-consultants to bring them leads.

What are your impressions of those entities and individuals who purchase your services?

When asked about the clients that purchase their services—in this case primarily other A/E/C firms—interviewees noted a lot of changes in recent years.

"They're becoming more like purchasing agents," said the vice president of a Pennsylvania-based MEP firm. "Today, more and more, services are acquired as commodities. They are looking only for the lowest fee."

At WorkingBuildings they agree that in most cases clients are looking to do more with less. Andrew Weinberg commentd: "The key is to best meet their goals in the most cost-effective manner possible, while at the same time making them look good to their constituents. The best clients are those that hire experts, and allow them to be the experts. Otherwise project quality suffers."

Pat McClave concurred: "Fee is the bottom line, which is a problem because you get what you pay for." Furthermore, he noted that, "Clients feel they give you a project and that is a reward. They have the attitude of 'what else do you want from us,' and yet they demand above and beyond the scope of work."

"Three prices." That was how Terry Kilbourne described his impressions of buyers, reinforcing another comment that clients are acting like purchasing agents.

Ryan Konst seeks out knowledgeable purchasers of his firm's services. He said, "The educated clients truly understand the value of our services, but there are those who treat our services as a commodity and they go to the lowest bidder every time." In fact, he segments clients by those who understand the value of good service, and those who look at his company as "a necessary evil or commodity."

This is where the intersection of business development, operations, and clients lies, according to Konst: "Good business development results in great relationships that mitigate the commoditization of consultants."

Participants at the 2012 Build Business research roundtable grappled with the extremely difficult position that sub-consultants are being placed in by their clients.

On one hand, many architecture, engineering, or construction firms are viewing their sub-consultants as a commodity, and treating them as such. On the other hand, the owners or end-users are demanding transparency.

Owners are more sophisticated and want to interact directly with sub-consultants. So there is a mix of decreased scopes of work coupled with increased needs from owners. Firms must learn to speak the owner's language, and advocate for them, without damaging the relationships with the architect, engineer, or constructor that hired them.

Specialty consultant Acoustics Dimensions has been able to avoid the commodity trend even though their core services have largely become commoditized. Noted Cathy Hutchison, "Some design-builders are giving away the services we provide." However, while Acoustic Dimensions continues to offer those services, they've been able to elevate their game and, when necessary, change the game.

"We have a very intentional focus to be the best, and to work with some of the top firms in the industry, offering a very collaborative approach. Our design clients like us, and we are dedicated to building long-term relationships that make money for both sides," said Hutchison.

Loyalty, or lack thereof, was cited by several interviewees. Terry Kilbourne believes that this is the single most significant thing that has changed among purchasers of his firm's services.

An executive from a full-service engineering firm in the mid-Atlantic region is frustrated with the lack of loyalty. "We have one architect that we've worked with a lot, but for one specific client. We have a great relationship. They often come to us when they are pursing work for other clients, but they always fee shop. And we always lose. So even though they like working with us, and tell us that we are the best engineer they work with, it really doesn't matter at the end of the day."

A number of participants shared scenarios in which they were asked by a client to put together some upfront programming and planning documents for a project, and the client turned around and gave the documents to other firms to price. Whereas the interviewees believed they had a sole-source opportunity for which they had put a lot of thought into, suddenly there were four or five competitors who were all in possession of the firm's planning documents.

This trend has an impact on both prime and sub-consulting firms. For sub-consultants it can actually take two forms: they may be part of a larger team doing the front-end work for the ultimate client (owner), or they may be doing the work for a prime firm, and be forced to compete against other similar sub-consultants.

Terry Kilbourne believes that relevant experience now outweighs established relationships: "Clients look for more specific experience, rather than go with who they always go with." He also noted an interesting change at architectural firms: "Surprisingly, a lot of younger staff are having increasing responsibility to do an initial review of who they want to use for engineering. Senior level staff still make decisions, but the younger staff now have more say, gaining more responsibilities earlier in their careers."

Steve Osborn believes that the buyers of his services are under a lot of pressure: "They have a big job, made even more complex in the past few years because of more consultants pursuing less available work and a lot of companies knocking on their doors."

Osborn also noted that A/E/C teams increasingly have to provide guidance on creative financing, because owners are facing the pressure of needing projects, but having limited capital.

Another point brought up by several participants was the increasingly-difficult insurance and liability requirements. For example, one firm pursuing a project with a $25,000 fee was forced to have professionally liability of $1 million per occurrence with a $3 million aggregate. Another noted absurd requirements for automotive and general liability insurance forcing him to make a decision of whether to increase the firm's coverage or walk away from opportunities.

Indemnification clauses have also become a sticking point in contract language, with clients demanding that firms accept the terms, claiming that other firms have worked under the terms. This stands in contrast to the advice of attorneys and liability insurance carriers that emphatically state, "Don't you dare sign that contract." Sub-consultants increasingly feel stuck in the middle, unsure of what to do. They need the work, but how much risk are they willing to accept to get the project?

An interesting geographic difference was demonstrated, anecdotally, during the research. Participants from multiple regions spoke of the difficulty in getting paid because they are "downstream" in the money flow. Several noted that they have been forced to call owners—as opposed to their A/E/C clients—to ask if funds had been released, circumventing their A/E/C clients, which puts them in an awkward position.

In one region, a participant noted that it is very difficult for new engineering firms to gain traction because, "All the architects owe the engineers so much money, that they keep going back to the same firms in an attempt to slowly make it up." But an interviewee in another geographic region shared a similar story about engineers having trouble getting paid by their architectural clients, but stating that, "The architects get so far in the hole that they stop using the firms they owe the most money to, and move on to other firms that haven't worked for them."

Conclusions and Summary

One overriding lesson learned during the research process is that sub-consultants and specialty consultants must think like prime professionals.

Firms are increasingly marketing directly to owners. In some cases, they are looking to gain new opportunities working under a prime contract. In other cases, they are trying to position themselves to be on teams, angling for a recommendation from the owner to a prime, or at least hoping to gain knowledge that would make the sub-consultant more competitive and attractive to a prime.

Relationships are as critical as they have ever been, and most firms are focusing on expanding their relationships with existing clients. However, there is also a trend away from loyalty, as many interviewees reported that formerly good clients are now treating them like a commodity. Their contracted scope is getting squeezed, lowest fee is ruling the day, and yet they are continually asked to do more.

There is no consensus about who should or will be doing business development. Many firms are moving toward the seller-doer model, because it reduces overhead and provides instant upfront technical value in the sales process. Yet other firms have brought in dedicated business development staff and have found the position to be of great benefit to their firms.

Tried and true marketing techniques are still being used by sub-consulting firms, but their overall processes are evolving. Some are placing a greater focus on becoming active in professional organizations and even local chambers of commerce. Others are aggressively moving forward with electronic marketing initiatives including blogs and social media. Several interviewees indicated that they are implementing CRM software, a practice more common with prime professionals. The importance of expanding and better utilizing networks was a consistent theme.

Firms have reacted differently with their target markets. Some have needed to diversify services or expand geographically. Others, however, have substantially narrowed their prospect lists to have a laser-like focus on only the most attractive potential clients.

Interviewees reported that the schedule demands have changed significantly, and they are increasingly being required to turn proposals and project deliverables around in almost unrealistic timeframes.

Interestingly, when asked about future trends that would impact their business, most sub-consultants did not mention major industry trends like Building Information Modeling, evidence-based design, sustainability, or integrated project delivery. Only a few interviewees mentioned one or more of these trends, though a change in the definition of "client" was mentioned by several participants. Sub-consulting firms are spending less time targeting architects and more time selling to contractors and construction managers.

Views toward clients were varied, as some interviewees reported that their clients were now acting like purchasing agents, while others were more sympathetic to the challenges facing their clients. There seemed to be a general desire, even longing, for more of a collaborative process, though only a few interviewees reported that as the norm for their firms. Increasingly stringent contractual requirements were cited by several people. Examples included excessive liability insurance requirements and unacceptable indemnification clauses.

Best Practices

What value is this information to a sub-consultant or specialty consultant? Here are a few recommended best practices.

Think like a prime. Combine marketing efforts to A/E/C prime firms with business development directed at owners. This will help position you to be a member of a project team, and may lead to direct work for the owner.

Think beyond your disciplines. Be aware of the trends impacting the prime firms you work for, as well as the issues that impact the owners. You need to speak the language of both in order to become a valuable member of the team.

Train your technical staff to become better business developers. Owners are expecting technical conversations very early in the sales process, and your key technical staff have a major role to play.

Invest in new marketing technologies, whether they relate to having a more robust online presence through websites and social media, or internal software like CRM programs.

Specialize and build your credentials for those particular services or target markets. Relationships will get you part-way there, but to be attractive to a prime professional you must have a depth of experience related to the specific opportunity you are chasing.

Diversify, but do so only in a way that makes sense for your firm. Don't abandon your core services, but find complementary services that you could offer to your existing clients.

Focus on your clients and work to develop business with existing accounts by providing new services, or by working at other client locations or facilities. Continually maintain contact with those clients that have no current work for your firm, and strive to be a source of education and knowledge to prospects, clients, and owners.

Pay more attention to the major trends impacting prime professionals or contractors with whom you work. If they are embracing evidence-based design, building information modeling, or integrated project delivery, chances are they will only hire sub-consultants that share the same outlook.

4 JACKS OF ALL TRADES
Multi-discipline Design and Planning

Researchers/Authors: Colleen Kucera, CPSM; Barbara Shuck, FSMPS, CPSM

Analysts/Editors: Emily Crandall, CPSM; Kim Icenhower, FSMPS, CPSM

Definition
This chapter research focused on multi-discipline seller firms that demonstrated diversity in numbers of employees, locations, number, and type of disciplines. Some firms declined to share strategies and insights.

Research Design
The research is based on discussions with eight individuals from six firms from August through October of 2012. The interviews were held in person, over the telephone, and via electronic means. Information from the Thought Leadership session at the 2012 Build Business, SMPS National Conference was also included.

What are your most effective current strategies and approaches to business development as you seek to provide design services?
The strategies most often used included thought leadership methods, relationship management, and strategic planning.

Thought Leadership

Thought leadership is a growing trend in the A/E/C community. It is being used to solidify relationships with current clients, attract new clients, and enhance client-focused collaboration. Thought leadership also builds brand recognition.

Thought leadership is a key business development strategy. Staff with deep knowledge and insights in core practice areas share innovative ideas and become industry leaders. Technical professionals who consult with clients on the front end of projects, often help clients to make informed decisions before a project is too far along. Sharing thought leadership at early stages can prevent costly changes and lengthy approval processes.

Employees at Perkins Eastman, an international planning, design, and consulting firm, publish books and articles within core practice areas that clearly distinguish themselves as industry thought leaders. Perkins Eastman uses thought leadership strategies with client panels and industry events. They leverage current client relationships to create new opportunities with clients they want to know. Panels and industry events provide an effective forum to mix old and new clients together, while sharing Perkins Eastman expertise and brand as thought leaders.

Wilson & Company Engineers & Architects, a multi-disciplinary engineering, architecture, surveying, mapping, environmental, and planning firm, also hosts technical workshops and focuses on thought leaders as part of their "Higher Relationships" company philosophy, which is based on their core values of "Shared Ownership, Collaboration, Intensity, Discipline, and Solutions." Topics relate to issues and concerns that clients face and they host workshops or present in client offices. Wilson & Company thought leaders write papers for technical journals, and are compensated accordingly for local, regional, and national publications.

Managing Relationships

Effective business development strategies for Wilson & Company focus on retaining clients, which involves periodic meetings and conducting client surveys, where professionals ask "how are we doing?" and "what could we do better?" The firm also hosts golf tournaments and staff attends trade shows so clients recognize the firm and network with project managers.

"We intend to stick to our brand and live our brand," said Cheryl Everitt, former Corporate Communications Manager for Wilson & Company. "In a multi-discipline firm, we have to shift resources and personnel on a moving target. We need to be very dynamic."

Everitt acknowledges that their current strategies are effective, and vary by target markets, where they divide their efforts into two categories: retaining clients and getting new ones. "We position ourselves to be the consulting firm of choice with all our clients," she said. "We really value our clients and focus on the 80 percent of where we typically get work. We're looking further out for project opportunities now, even a couple of years."

Two markets, rail and petrochemical, have entirely different business development approaches because clients are private. Project managers have recurring face-to-face contact to keep at the top of clients' minds.

Although every client is different, many projects are won based on relationship and competitive fee among a select list of consulting firms. Everitt said that they are seeing fewer firms being asked to the table, as well as more sensitivity to project costs. Within the infrastructure discipline, which has traditionally been private developer-driven, managing relationships is the most effective way to be added to requests for bid lists. "The economy has put a lot of A's (architects) and E's (engineers) out of work, so we're competing against some who are working out of their garages," she said. "It is sometimes hard to compete."

Burns & McDonnell has 3,700 employees that serve eleven internal global practices nationwide. Bryan Hughes, business development manager, has been with Burns & McDonnell for two years. He has one support staff member in his office, and he manages business development efforts for seven disciplines in the California office. Fortunately, he has effectively no limits with regard to travel within the company's corporate and regional office locations, which makes it easier for him to work with other offices and develop in-house partnerships.

"People will help you, especially if you sit down with them and build trust, face-to-face," said Hughes. "That's very important." Each discipline and regional office operates independently, as its own profit center. The company uses various business development models: seller-doer (technical staff responsibility, in addition to billable work), business development professionals, and a hybrid model that combines the two.

Pennoni Associates (Pennoni) is a multi-discipline engineering firm with more than 900 employees in twenty-eight offices. Their business development focus is primarily based on relationships and reputation, with 85 to 90 percent of their work being repeat business.

"This business is all about relationships and reputation, and guarding those relationships is a very big piece of what we do every day," said David DeLizza, PE, Senior Vice President, and Strategic Growth. Melissa Rysak is Associate Vice President, Director of Corporate Communications, and Aimee Lala is former Strategic Communications Manager.

Pennoni has client coordinators, whose role, in addition to getting technical work done, is to maintain the business relationship. That goes from developing new opportunities, to making sure the bills go out, to making sure the cash comes in.

"We really try to make sure that the client coordinators are managing the big-picture relationship with their best clients," DeLizza said.

"When I see the kinds of things that Melissa and Aimee talk about in SMPS, these are the kinds of things we want to teach all of our people. Those of us who grew up at Pennoni, we know this, and now it's our job to take the opportunity and responsibility to push it down the line to other managers."

"Some of the client coordinators are part of the marketing staff, and there are others who are from the technical staff who have shown more of a business development acumen to have a development role as part of their status, so that varies from client to client," said Lala. "Most of the client coordinators start out as technical staff, but there are also those who start out in business development, then turn the potential client over to a technical staff person, and then go on and look for the next opportunity."

Planning: Strategy, Business Development, Capture Plans, etc.

Communication, collaboration, and setting realistic goals are part of the Perkins Eastman culture. Every year, all practice leaders convene for a strategic planning meeting, which provides one new idea that will be implemented for the upcoming fiscal year.

Dibble Engineering (Dibble) is a multi-discipline engineering firm that has one business development director, one marketing professional, and a corporate relations professional who focuses on the political side of the business. There is also one firm principal who is focused on and oversees business development, and another who focuses on marketing.

Each practice has its own business plan and there is a company-wide strategic plan, which encompasses general company initiatives. Practice leaders split their time between business development (about 30 percent) and billable work (about 70 percent). The business development director works with each practice leader to bring in new work and retain existing clients. Dibble has found that clients prefer to speak to the technical staff who will actually be doing the work. The business development director helps open doors to new business, maintains existing clients, and acts as a conductor to orchestrate all the practices in their business development activities and initiatives.

Dibble uses a formalized capture plan very early on in a pursuit, which has become more flexible due to the changing economy. They are seeing more surprise projects, either by funding being suddenly added, or, more often, projects being removed or reduced, according to Stephanie Muñoz, Business Development Director.

HOK, a global design, architecture, engineering, and planning firm has many key clients, however, they work to identify the top fifty opportunities for winning new clients and work each year. They work to have executive committee knowledge of those opportunities and track them through the chief marketing officer and the marketing board. Some of these clients are shared between multiple offices, while others are specific to a particular office location.

All major HOK offices have a marketing principal who oversees both business development and marketing, and a marketing manager who reports to the principal. There may be marketing coordinators and business development professionals within this structure, depending on office size. The five major business units each have a national business development and marketing staff. The main focus is on these five units, and the firm also pursues other miscellaneous work. Each office also has a seller/doer model.

Business development at HOK focuses on winning work for all the disciplines within each office. Not every office has all disciplines and some offices are significantly stronger than others in a certain business unit. For example, Los Angeles is one of the top offices for health care and aviation. Chicago and St. Louis are strong in justice. When pursuing local work within a business unit, the national and local business development people collaborate closely throughout the pursuit. Landscape architecture, engineering, and consulting services can also do work for other firms and are not tied to only completing work that HOK has designed.

DeLizza described Pennoni's bi-annual meetings, where about 100 managers meet off-site for business planning, including discussions on how they did fiscally last year, and how they are doing so far this year. The fall program focuses on professional development and project management training, and some senior management and staff give presentations on various efforts they're working on.

Rysak said the firm is trying to make sure that employees are attentive and engaged in everything they are doing. "We are transparent as far as letting them know where our initiatives are, where our goals are. We have an employee portal where a lot of that information resides. We get the message out loud and clear so everyone knows where they fit in."

How effective are your current strategies and approaches to business development, and do you see them changing in the future?

Firms are focusing on creating better seller-doers and training staff to be better equipped to handle the seller activities, including more cooperation and collaboration between marketing and business development.

The current business climate is extremely competitive and firms did not see this changing. Being flexible with service delivery methods, teaming, and internal coordination is imperative to remaining competitive.

Continue Focus on Technical Expertise

Something that Wilson & Company does not see changing is how to leverage existing work and retain existing clients through the efforts of their thought leaders. "We are creating new thought leaders in new areas," Cheryl Everitt said. "All of those things will create a strategic business approach in the future. As projects are more complex, project managers must become better businesspeople," she said. "They need to manage teams better and progress to senior project manager, which involves more business development skills. Marketing is becoming its own discipline," she said. "Our project managers are more responsible and the whole process is more sophisticated with multiple audiences and more geographic diversity."

More Marketing and Business Development Collaboration

There is no sales or business development structure that crosses profit center lines within Burns & McDonnell, and each practice has no mandated connection to the rest of the company for business development or marketing strategy. Hughes stated, "I think coordination of business development and marketing between profit centers will be one of the fundamental challenges going forward."

Currently each practice has its own business development process that is based on client profile, needs, and historical methodology. "We are a highly entrepreneurial firm that allows the maximum flexibility to each practice/office. Each has a different method to sell services, which makes it extraordinarily difficult," he said.

As the firm's business development professional, he overlaps, and in some cases, conflicts with the sales interests of other practices/offices. "In my case, I am basically a resource to the practices seeking to build business in my regional office. As such, I have no goals, no measurables," he said.

"There's competition for my time when there's a lot going on. The discipline leaders all feel they need local dedication and support. Since every office approaches business development in a different manner, each has its own positioning, go/no-go, and proposal kick-off processes. Sometimes the global practice business developer alerts the local office leader of opportunities, and sometimes they don't. Local involvement varies widely. In some cases, the global practice marketing lead will assume responsibility for a lead generated by the regional office," said Hughes.

Less Predictable and Reliable

Dibble focuses primarily on the public market sector, which used to be very predictable with Capital Improvement Plans (CIP) being readily available. Now the CIP reports are not as reliable, causing Dibble to have to be more fluid.

Stay Strong To Brand and Reputation

AMI has a special service offering: providing healthier buildings and safe working environments. The ARID team uses the same business development messages and communication strategies for website development, social media, promotional campaigns, etc. "Our goal is educating and helping clients create better buildings," said Melissa Scaturro.

Pennoni's strategy of keeping their eye on their goals will not change. David DeLizza said, "Our annual business goals are very simple: 'Excellent Professional Reputation, Profit and Growth.' These were the goals when Chuck Pennoni founded the firm in 1966. He used to say, 'If you don't have a reputation in this business, you're not going anywhere.'"

They get strategic direction from Tony Bartolomeo, President of Pennoni, according to Rysak. "He's always ten steps ahead of where we are today, and knows what's coming up. And also, making sure we follow Mr. Pennoni's philosophy—that the client comes first, our reputation is paramount, having a vision of what's coming up, and knowing what the next big thing is—Dave has a good framework to build the strategic plan from to make it work."

HOK has seen definite downward pressure on their fees. "Some firms have been taking huge risks with their fees such as 0 percent profit, but that is not the business that HOK is in," said Elaine Kanelos, Vice President, Director of Strategic Development. HOK has been very strategic about fee structures to stay competitive, but they are not trying to buy jobs.

Remain Client-Centric

"You can trace the company's method back to Chuck Pennoni, who has a very client-centric attitude at all times," said Rysak. "It isn't a matter of whether we can give the client what they need, it's a matter of how do we get them what they need. I see that DeLizza has been given the freedom to follow his instincts about how best to serve our clients. And the best way to serve our existing municipal infrastructure base is being financially solid and being able to continue to provide them with the work they are expecting from us, and not have to pull people from projects because you've had to lay off staff from other areas, but to be solid. That's how we serve the 85 percent. How we serve the other 15 percent is by constantly evolving and changing and offering new things."

There has been a national focus within HOK to train the project managers and project architects on business development techniques, with specific focus on key individuals with significant client interaction. HOK Los Angeles has been hosting industry events at their office for firm visibility, in addition to supporting their goal of becoming a better community member.

How have you changed your strategies and approaches to business development in recent years, and do you see these changes as short term or permanent?

Most firms interviewed spoke about service innovation and how it continues to distinguish firms, from making key hires with specialized technical expertise, to embracing new project delivery processes.

Another development that Perkins Eastman has created over the last five years is a strategic consulting group where experts who are not architecturally trained bring their strong backgrounds in strategy development and the environment to the table. Workplace, health care, senior living, and educational environments are all members of the strategies group, along with an approach to large scale city issues that integrates urban design, urban planning, landscape, and urban economics.

Dibble changed strategies by investing in the land development market prior to the economy coming back full force, so they are entrenched when the market is ready. The firm is already seeing positive signs and market improvement. Another change in strategy for Dibble has been to move to more of a full-service selling approach, where they are cross-selling services between their eight practices.

One of the AMI business development initiatives was to bring in a key hire with expertise that brought added value and a new testing service to AMI clients. "We wanted to push the market, and we knew that we could do that to create awareness of the person as an expert," said Melissa Scaturro, Business Development Director.

"We were looking for a person who could bring experience so we could expand based on our plan to grow those capabilities. He understands it's important for him, and he's very willing to work with us to create advertising pieces to send out to existing clients to expand our reach."

ARID leadership continues to monitor AMI's key hire strategy to determine if it would be advantageous for them.

Another successful result from sharing marketing resources improves client strategies, where information is beneficial for both. "In a niche market, our special expertise is very critical," said Scaturro. "Sharing strategy, insights, leads, client hot buttons, and preferences enhances opportunities for winning more work and improving client satisfaction."

"One of the other strategic things we did about a year and a half ago is that we made an acquisition, and as a result of that transition, we've reorganized our firm into regions," said Lala. Existing regional vice presidents run those regions.

"We had everybody in house already. We just shuffled the cards and put people in the best possible roles they could be in, and that streamlines a lot," she said. "With strategic growth meetings, everyone knew exactly what their roles were and what they would focus on."

"That was a change that happened short-term, but it had long-term impacts," said Rysak. It has tested out positively. "We've had to allow our structures to be fluid, to be able to adjust to new markets and new initiatives. Aimee's role is a good example. We realized there were some holes after the reorganization. Everyone had newly-assigned responsibilities. Now we're filling in the cracks so every role is optimized."

According to Melissa Rysak, Pennoni has had a strong federal presence for many years, which was further bolstered by a recent acquisition that also had a strong federal portfolio. The acquired firm was very successful in the federal arena, but was not able to provide the breadth of services that Pennoni can. "I remember their vice president who ran their federal efforts saying, 'Melissa, I'm just a kid in a candy store to be part of the Pennoni team.' To someone who just inherited all these new disciplines to service his clients with, he saw the amazing benefit in the pursuit of federal work to have all those disciplines in house."

"The main thing with these initiatives is to start them up, grow them, make them profitable, and once they're profitable, push them into operations, and then pick up another initiative and do the same," said David DeLizza. "That is the way to grow."

Strategic Teaming Is an Effective Approach, Even though Firms Have Multiple Disciplines In-House

Strategically, Burns & McDonnell seeks to marry technical strengths with client needs and may pull in a team from another firm to win work. Teaming has been an effective response to the economic downturn, especially within the regional office group. The decision to team is relationship-driven. "As a relatively new player in a market, strategic teaming is often the most successful entry point," Hughes said. In his geographic region he reported, "Burns & McDonnell clients frequently have high disadvantaged business enterprise (DBE) requirements (up to 40 percent), which forces teaming strategies."

Be Different and Create More Face-to-Face Time

Perkins Eastman has developed a creative way to gain new clients in response to the economic downturn. They organized eight different "Think Tanks" across the country with approximately ten to twelve industry leaders and consultants. Of the industry leaders invited, approximately half were current or past clients. The other half were new or potential clients. The results of these Think Tanks were presented at the American Association of Homes & Services for the Aging (now Leading Age) annual meeting in November 2010. This resulted in new relationships, reinforcement of thought leadership positioning, and contributing to innovation in the industry. The Think Tank idea came from the 2009 meeting for the senior living group.

Strategies in all disciplines migrate from general marketing, branding, and promotional messages to face-to-face meetings and business development tactics when there is a specific project on the horizon. This allows firms to understand the mission and objectives of a project so issue-specific proposals will resonate better with the audience. Wilson & Company is using Twitter to communicate with specific markets, and are seeing the value of social media for specific target marketing.

Rysak points out that many of their initiatives are non-traditional. "Civil engineers don't go into energy; and civil engineers don't go into design-build, or into oil and gas," she said.

"DeLizza needs to be given a lot of credit for leading the company into non-traditional initiatives. We're the engineering world's equivalent of the shiny new toy everybody wants to see. It's an awe factor. When I'm talking to people and tell them that we lead design-build efforts as an engineer, they're just floored with it. Civil engineers don't get bonded. They just don't. Our firm has trusted DeLizza to take the route that's not as safe to take, and it has paid off for us."

Lala adds, "It's interesting to see the thought process. Take oil and gas. They're drilling gas out of the ground, and they need roads to get there, which is civil engineering. We take the skillsets that we have, and apply it to the markets that are growing right now. That's another thing that sets us apart. We see where the markets are going and determine what engineering they are going to need to make that work ."

"We're a civil engineering firm that does x, y, and z," said Rysak. "That's my push right now, to explain to everyone that Pennoni is a civil engineering firm that does x, y, and z. We're not an oil and gas firm, we're not an energy firm, and we're not an MEP firm. We're a civil engineering firm that does x, y, and z. We remain true to our roots, and Aimee had a wonderful point: the main source of income we've had in oil and gas is infrastructure, doing the roadways to help the big companies get their trucks from A to B. That is not how the rest of the companies in Pennsylvania are making their shale money. We took our civil engineering skillset and applied it to the market. We do a lot of non-civil engineering disciplines, like survey, testing, inspections, but in our hearts, that's what we are. So there are very non-traditional roots we're digging in."

Gathering statistical information, measuring results, and managing data is an ever-increasing business skill, and should not be foreign to A/E/C professionals of all areas of expertise.

Everitt agrees that Wilson & Company still struggles with integrating multiple disciplines for a combined project pursuit. "Sharing work across the company is more difficult now," she said. "For example, if we need MEP to work for a rail client, we submit a quote on the work, and often pricing is based on local conditions, where our MEP may not have the local expertise and pricing experience. We are working through a better cost structure strategy. We may not be able to cross-sell the discipline if the pricing is not competitive."

Wilson & Company closely tracks utilization rates, and looks for internal teaming opportunities where rates may not be as sensitive. "We just may not be able to compete," she said. Pushing their services into other markets may not be effective after additional analysis. They are considering adapting additional pricing strategies due to fluctuations in the economy.

In all instances, they are hesitant to put a client relationship at risk. In some developer projects, they have resources to provide full services, where they would be more competitive if they worked directly with the developer, instead of serving as a sub-consultant to the developer. Their focus on maintaining client relationships sometimes results in delivering fewer services across geographic areas, which negates the benefit of being a diversified, multi-discipline firm.

As for responding to economic changes, Pennoni is looking at how they have done things in the past, and how they can streamline and save money, according to Rysak. "Instead of trying to retract new initiatives, we're trying to cut spending and improve efficiencies in areas that we were already in, for example, our trade shows. One of the things that Lala is responsible for is looking at our trade show investments and how to better track—and then increase—our return on investment. Using information that I learned at SMPS University, I realized that we needed to better manage follow-ups and pre- and post-show marketing efforts. Lala's responsibility is to make sure we're maximizing our trade show investments. By saving money in our trade shows, and making better use of our investment, we will hopefully have some recaptured revenues that can be reinvested in some other initiatives."

With forty-two trade shows per year that were previously coordinated by technical and business development staff, Lala, an experienced business developer herself, is providing enhanced value through cross-selling and sharing more of the Pennoni story. "Because I'm big picture, I can help them tell a better story." Rysak said that while trade shows may not be a huge investment in a lot of firms, it is a $250,000 per year expenditure at Pennoni and now they can manage their efforts more effectively.

HOK has adapted strategies and approaches in recent years. The firm has an increasingly strong go/no-go process, where pursuing projects when they have not previously been in contact with the client is discouraged. "There must be a compelling reason to pursue a project they have not pre-positioned for, and it is becoming rarer that they pursue those types of projects," said Kanelos.

Shift in Targeted Business Development

HOK's business development efforts are client-focused, rather than project-focused. This has been a more recent change but it is being embraced throughout the firm. Their five business units have remained the same even with the change from project- to client-focused.

Business development has put more of an emphasis on continued client relationships after a project has been completed. A formalized process for this has not been developed, but with the shift from project-focused to client-focused business development, this is becoming more top of mind.

Another change is that HOK has put a heavier focus on becoming a strong community member within their local environments.

What changes do you plan to make in the future regarding either strategy or approach to business development, and do you see these changes as short term or permanent?

Project managers must improve general business skills, especially the development of long-term client relationships and communications, instead of relying on technical expertise to succeed in their careers.

Looking forward, David Hoglund, President of Perkins Eastman, predicts that identifying and training future leaders will result in enhanced client service. Perkins Eastman is investing in a pilot program for standouts who will have leadership shadowing opportunities with marketing and business development education, which bodes well for understanding how to effectively communicate and leverage firm expertise. "Clients do not want their project to be a training ground for your firm," he said.

"We will have to see," said Everitt, regarding how strategies will change in the future. "They are not as effective as they used to be, when it was relationship, relationship, relationship. It doesn't supply Wilson & Company with a long-term strategy anymore," she said. "Employees leave, clients leave, and relationships aren't as strong as they were in previous years. It doesn't make as much difference if we don't have long-term employees. To rely solely on relationships is a false hope in the coming years." When employees leave, they may go work for competitors.

For that reason, Wilson & Company is emphasizing their "Higher Relationship" brand position in the marketplace and their commitment to core values. "To focus on new segments, you have to bring the brand with you, and they don't know who you are," she said. "Our project managers are individuals, and they represent what the company stands for. For big dollar purchases, we see that clients would prefer to go with the brand, and the project manager has to act like the salesman. The client can't afford to take a chance on just the individual relationship."

"For scopes and fees, it's just plain good business to be flexible," Everitt said. For example, there was a Wilson & Company client who wanted more services for less. "If we could have, we would have sharpened our pencil, and then we would have lost money. We need to communicate." Scoping and feeing projects effectively must be specific about what the client is not going to get. Before the economic downturn it wasn't specific. "We have had to learn and not be sloppy," she said.

Hughes anticipates Burns & McDonnell using an "all of the above" approach to business development strategies in the foreseeable future.

> "It's less of a 'we can do it all' mentality and more 'leverage what we do really well,'" said Hughes of Burns & McDonnell.

Hughes recommends not to accept company culture for what it is, and to try new initiatives and efforts to enhance business development across organizational constraints. He also recommends building bridges internally. "If you don't, you won't have them when you need them," he said. "Remove obstacles, and break down barriers at every opportunity." He said he has noticed that younger employees don't accept perceived barriers in the workplace the same as older employees. "Not communicating is no longer acceptable," he said.

Dibble is adapting the way they do business because clients are changing employees quickly through cutbacks and retirements, just as A/E/C firms have seen turnover. Staff are spending more time on client education where they are assisting their clients in process and procedures, often times teaching them about the industry and their own organization.

Client access has become more difficult. Clients that used to be open to meetings are no longer willing to be as available for appointments. They have worked around this by getting more involved in philanthropy, professional associations, and public meetings where they know their clients will be in attendance. Dibble will continue to have senior project managers develop client relationships, join industry organizations, and focus more on business development efforts in the future. The importance of business development and marketing working together will continue to become more pivotal in winning work.

Originally, ARID served residential and commercial clients, and leaders foresaw an economic downturn and diversified accordingly. They currently serve almost an entirely commercial client base, and have found the work to be more stable, depending on large general contractors and repeat work, contrasted with the short "in and out" of residential work.

"You have to listen for opportunities both ways," Melissa Scaturro said. "It's much easier now that ARID is commercial." She has a two-person marketing department, which is shared between the two firms. The AMI website was recently updated, and she intends to do the same with ARID. "I want to get the process and flow going first for AMI," she said.

"One of Pennoni's marketing challenges is that we don't want to be anything besides a civil engineering firm. But, we want to be a civil engineering firm that does a lot of different things. We want to take these things that we've been doing and make sure that people know about them to potentially lead to more work. But we have to do that in a way that doesn't change our reputation or stray too far away from being a civil engineering firm. As our business development is evolving, we have to find ways to market our new service lines without fundamentally changing who we are," Rysak said.

Another Pennoni initiative is design-build. About two years ago, they recognized the amount of design-build activity, and have done a lot of work as a sub-consultant to an architect or contractor. After looking at the market trends, however, they realized they were not maximizing design-build opportunities and decided to flip the traditional design-build model.

"We have our own bonding capacity, and can take the lead role in design-build projects," said DeLizza. "Many firms would never do that. Our bonding agent gave us a $10 million per project limit, and a $25 million aggregate. Since taking this route, we've done some design-build projects where we are the lead.

"So on the design-build side, we're trying to get more of our client base to consider us doing design-build projects with them. It's part of the sales pitch: one entity as opposed to an architect, a contractor, and several engineers, seven or eight contracts, one source of responsibility with the financial ability to do a contract," DeLizza said.

Pennoni has a five year strategic plan in place with a goal of $170 million in gross revenues by 2016. Current revenues are about $120 million. With a strong base of existing clients, some of their business lines do well, and they are considering mergers, acquisitions, and new business lines, like oil and gas. They don't believe they will need to add staff as they have in-house expertise, which is another advantage because cash outlay is minimized with the people already sitting somewhere in the organization.

DeLizza said they plan for the long-term, but they remain "stealthy and fluid." Business conditions can change daily, especially with the energy market, for example. We've got to be in the position to be very flexible, and I think our clients recognize that. When we were preparing our strategic plan, our engineers wanted a lot more detail, but we thought it should be flexible and in plain English."

Rysak adds that the plan is specific enough that they know where they're going, but not so specific that it pigeon-holes the firm. They allow for a case by case decision-making process as long as the outcome benefits the success of the strategic plan.

Another Pennoni initiative is international growth. They have some international work, and are now looking at more opportunities: large planning and design projects. They see the international market as an opportunity to do the same as in the United States, and they also understand risks that are involved, so they are looking at them on a case-by-case basis.

"HOK continues to research and evolve to develop business development strategies and approaches in the ever-changing world," said Kanelos. In 2011, HOK hired their first chief marketing officer whose focus is on process, strategy, and winning more work. All of the changes that HOK has made in response to economic changes are permanent changes for the firm. "The world has changed and we are not going back," said Kanelos.

As you look forward to the next ten years, what trends and considerations will most influence how you conduct business development to offer design and construction services?

During the next ten years, Perkins Eastman will continue its focus on collaborative strategies, thought leadership, and service innovation, according Hoglund. "Expertise-driven firms cannot afford to 'silo' expertise as new building types evolve that straddle multiple building types. Hospitality design has informed new models of senior living, while health care education is evolving from academic medical centers into allied health models that bring research, learning, and health care career education together. Age-friendly cities understand the importance of integrating transportation, housing, retail, hotel, educational, and commercial uses to create vibrant downtown centers," said Hoglund. Finally, he sees a continued trend for firms to stay on their toes and go into a project with the very best fee and a sharp pencil. "Firms do not want services to become a commodity item."

Wilson & Company sees project delivery changing in the future, with design-build, public private participation, joint ventures, and set-asides. Everitt said, "We are figuring out ways of joining forces with others to get the work, which includes training and using different project teaming structures. We see these to be huge issues in the future. As for design-build, it's a relatively new thing, and it's really important to our clients to show that we're being flexible to their preferences," she said. "If we're using design-build for a project, we must have the dexterity to take advantage of current situations. Our flexibility and dexterity will shift as the market shifts, although it's not too much different than a single-discipline firm."

According to Everitt, "In twenty to thirty recent proposals, clients are throwing out those who haven't already done the work, such as conceptual design. Design firms have already raised the bar, and I don't know how you slide back to the old way. We still have to show how we can solve the client's problem in the proposal."

"Today, Wilson & Company is more lean and mean, and has lowered its cost of doing business," she said. They are responding to changes in project delivery, and reflecting more effectively on client-driven needs. "We need to adapt to be efficient and effective," she said. "People don't' have money to design, bid and build projects inefficiently."

As they look to the future, Dibble's fully implemented CRM system, Deltek Vision, is more important than ever, and it will continue to be pushed throughout the firm.

"Knowledge is power and the historical information Deltek Vision provides is the best tool they have for procuring new business," said Muñoz. "It also helps in communicating throughout the company and in cross-selling services between practices."

The next ten years is full of opportunity at Pennoni. "We have a bunch of initiatives right now, including energy, building efficiency systems, energy audits, etc.," explained DeLizza. "What we're doing is trying to take a project from the audit phase all the way through to building the project for the client, and help them find an investor to fund the improvements—a turnkey approach."

"We are willing to put, in very select cases, our money where our mouth is. We're willing to come in and help them get the funding. Engineers typically don't play that role," said Rysak. "Our challenge is that we are a civil engineering firm, and for the people who know Pennoni, that's what they know."

Pennoni looks at maintaining its multi-discipline service line in the next 10 years. Lala is responsible to determine how to explain how we do everything we do through trade shows, proposals, and strategic teaming arrangements. These efforts cannot alienate 80 percent of their client base, which includes townships and municipal engineering clients. They're concerned about their traffic signal, and their township, and the shopping center they need built, and may not be interested in other Pennoni services. "We have to be a lot of things to a lot of people," said Rysak.

Kanelos said that the role of business development and marketing at HOK will continue to become more important within the industry and A/E/C firms. She sees that quantifying information is going to remain a critical component of business development. Putting metrics to measuring the firm's success is going to be crucial for business development and marketing. It is getting harder to be a middle-sized firm. Smaller firms are lean and extremely competitive with price. Larger firms can provide more bang for the buck with multiple disciplines, locations, and resources at their disposal any time. HOK feels this hasn't changed, but loyalty should go both directions.

Conclusion and Summary

Multi-discipline firms are slowly changing the way they work and while relationships are still important—they can be misleading if firms are not prepared for change, specifically the turnover rate at client organizations and peer organizations. The multi-discipline firms that remain true to core competencies and values are finding unique ways to provide services and develop business for existing clients. Firms need to be flexible in how and what services they provide and to which clients.

Most of the firms interviewed have a strong strategic planning process in place and are using that to guide future business development and marketing decisions. Thought leadership appears to be a trend among some of the firms. This trend originated almost twenty years ago and is now being embraced by A/E/C firms looking for a way to differentiate themselves in an ever-increasing competitive marketplace.

While all firms stated relationships were important and key to retaining existing clients, there was an underlying weakness when firms did not see staffing turnovers coming and were not prepared. The relationship dynamic is changing. Some client firms were difficult to get face time with so they are looking for professional and community organizations as a way to connect. While this may not seem like a new idea, for some firms it represents a new way to develop and maintain business.

Another effect of staff turnover is the need to educate clients and employees on the firm's business and sometimes the client's business. Explaining what is not included is as important as explaining what is included in the scope of work. Firms are being asked to do more with less.

Firms discussed strategic teaming to combat an increasingly competitive marketplace. An example of the flexibility is when a multi-discipline firm offers a service and then has to sub it out to meet pricing for a new job or client to remain profitable.

Best Practices

Companies are making a shift in business development that is more client-focused instead of project-focused.

Each discipline has its own clients, who have their specific needs, preferences, and relationships. These factors may not apply when selling across disciplines. However, firms that do not cross-sell are finding themselves at a disadvantage. This comes from not sharing information internally about client intelligence and trends that apply across disciplines.

Small firms have more flexibility to effectively and profitably integrate business development. Multi-discipline firms find that some departments are competing against very small firms with low overhead and a pricing advantage. Strategic teaming helps combat this trend.

Cross-selling services requires regular communication and a collaborative culture. Firms with a silo structure must begin to embrace communication at all levels, not just the principal level, to remain competitive. Successful business development requires flexibility, advocacy, strong internal relationships, and open-mindedness.

Try out new ideas and initiatives on disciplines that are more established, where working through technology and strategies will have the quickest impact leading to success. From adding key technical staff to testing website platforms and social media strategies, multi-discipline firms can benefit from shared costs and lessons learned.

Stable repeat business can provide profits that allow new initiatives to be undertaken. This means that taking care of existing clients should be an important part of a firm's business development model. Client firms and behavior is changing and firms need to be flexible to retain existing clients. Technical staff must embrace and be responsible for client relationship management. Serving clients well is still the best business development effort, but it is also expected. Firms need to talk to clients about future trends and discuss how to better serve these clients.

Strategic planning is foundational for focusing business development efforts. There is no magic strategic plan; they are as unique as each firm. However, firms that undertake the effort to look at more than just revenue are finding success.

Corporate communications and identity enhance a firm's brand, internally and externally.

5 DIRECTORS
Constructors and Construction Managers

Researchers/Authors: Edward Bond, Jr., FSMPS, FCMAA, LEED AP;
Scott W. Braley, FAIA, FRSA; Cricket Robertson, CPSM; Katie van der Sleesen

Analysts/Editors: Tracey Gould, MS, IMC; Cricket Robertson, CPSM

Definition
This chapter deals with construction and construction management firms who hold a contract directly with the owner.

Research Design
A series of qualitative interviews were conducted with senior business development and executive business development professionals from large, national and international, multi-disciplinary construction, construction management, and consulting firms that specialize in the design and construction industry. These professionals either currently, or recently, worked at these construction or construction management (CM) firms.

Due to the sensitivity of the material presented, each professional participated on the condition of anonymity. In respecting their wishes, all firm names have been removed. However, they will be referred to as the following five firms and respective interviewees.

Firm 1: Full-service consulting and training firm focused exclusively on the A/E/C industry.

Interviewee 1: Seasoned professional with thirty years of experience, national speaker, worked with ENR top-ranked firms both nationally and internationally.

Firm 2: National commercial contractor, more than 100 years of building experience, ENR top-tier-ranked contractor, private family-owned with Native American roots.

Interviewee 2: Certified business development professional, recipient of multiple industry awards and recognitions, active on multiple organization committees and boards of directors.

Firm 3: Business coaching firm coaching both senior leadership of hospitals, universities, and critical care facilities, and leadership teams of service providers.

Interviewee 3: Business development and marketing professional with more than thirty years of experience on both the service firm side, and the consulting and coaching side in the design and construction industries.

Firm 4: International, employee-owned construction firm with annual revenues exceeding $1 billion.

Interviewee 4: Business development and marketing professional with nearly twenty years of experience, national speaker.

Firm 5: International, privately-owned real-estate development construction firm, Fortune 100 best companies to work for.

Interviewee 5: National business development professional responsible for sales and marketing with more than twenty-two years of experience with the firm.

Questions

Interviews were conducted via telephone. In addition to the following five questions, and with their respective answers, each professional offered unstructured insight to their respective business development efforts and where they see our industry going in the next decade. Additionally, information presented at industry-specific conferences, gathered from participation in industry-specific surveys, and of other large contractors was also incorporated.

Baseline Research Questions

Each of the professionals interviewed were asked the same five baseline questions:

- What are your most effective, current strategies and approaches to business development, as you seek to provide construction/construction management services?
- How effective are your current strategies and approaches to business development, and how do you see them changing in the next ten years ahead?
- How have you changed your strategies and approaches to business development in recent years, and do you see these changes as short term or permanent in the decade ahead?
- What changes do you plan to make in the next ten years regarding either strategy or approach to business development, and do you see these changes as short term or permanent?

- As you look forward to the next ten years, what trends and considerations will most influence how you conduct business development to offer design and construction services?

Additional and Follow-up Questions

After discussing each of the five base questions, the following follow-up questions were asked.

- What are your networking tactics, and how are you staying in front of clients?
- Are you noticing downward trends in regards to certain activities/events?

When discussing questions with the interviewees, many of their answers applied to more than one question. In an effort to streamline the answers and not repeat any of the information in each response, the following results are a combination of the answers divided into common topics.

Strategies

Relationships, Relationships, Relationships

The phrase everyone hears in real estate is "location, location, location." That translates into "relationships, relationships, relationships" in the design and construction industry. Clients are getting smarter and more sophisticated, and they are realizing they are in the driver's seat.

More CMs are focusing on clients and not on projects; or in other words, moving from a pursuit strategy to a client strategy.

Creating those long-term relationships with your clients creates opportunity and is more likely to create a steady stream of projects, versus moving from project-to-project.

Large firms are benefiting from being able to follow their clients into multiple geographical markets, while helping their clients be successful at their business. Relationships aren't meant to be short-term; they won't be successful unless they are long-term. It's also important to remember that building relationships takes time—it doesn't happen overnight. You need to learn the client and their business so you can give them not only what they want, but what they need.

In today's marketplace, the objective is to get the job—not the RFP. Creating relationships and staying in front of the client will help you pre-sell and position yourself before an RFP "hits the street." When you are talking with the client, an important strategy is to blanket the client at multiple levels. Don't just send in your business development professionals and expect them to be solely responsible for building relationships. Instead, send in your executives, project directors, project managers, and superintendents as well. Each of your company's personnel needs to be reaching out to their respective peers on the client's side. The more you can be in touch with your client, the better. Successful CM firms are implementing client relationship accountability at multiple levels, and targeting clients where it matters most has the greatest impact.

Each client has hot buttons, or issues, that keep them awake at night. Knowing your client gives you the opportunity to learn those hot buttons and will help you customize your response to their specific needs. Interviewee 3 indicated that hot buttons are not always project specific. Instead, they are related to the client's business issues and strategy. Also, you need to differentiate yourself in the value you bring to the client and the unique solutions you have—largely because of the knowledge you have gained in creating your relationship. You can answer those unasked questions and provide solutions that help the client be successful in their business. In essence, tell them something they don't already know.

You also need to understand that it's never a level playing field. The winning firm will be the one with the relationship with the client. It's also important to know who the selection committee is, especially the main decision maker. There is always a main person who will have the ultimate say in firm award, and in order to win the project before the shortlist, relationships need to be clearly established and nurtured.

Owners are hiring the individuals they are going to work with for an extended amount of time for each project; they aren't hiring a company. When they are selecting those individuals they are going to be working with, they are more likely to choose people they know and trust, versus the people they don't. This is where having multiple layers of relationships plays a key role. Firms have learned that losing the relationship your project manager had with the last successful project is a waste. Leveraging those relationships—keeping that project manager in the relationship loop—is the key. This will also help with the next win, as they already know the client. The knowledge they have from the last project just might be the ace up your sleeve.

Once you have won a project or two, leverage those wins to win other clients and projects. This will not only help strengthen your current relationships, but it will help you build new relationships. It also speaks volumes about your capabilities and allows you to more easily sell your portfolio of experience across other sectors and markets.

Networking

The industry is seeing a shift away from spending large amounts of money on client entertainment. Interviewee 1 noticed tighter approval processes for this kind of spending. Company decision makers are requiring a substantial return on investment as part of the justification process. Firms are willing to participate in functions on a limited basis, as long as they can influence the people they will get face time with as a direct result of their involvement.

With the decrease in entertainment activities, business development professionals are spending more time and effort on participating in their clients' professional organizations. This participation goes beyond simply being a member of various organizations, but includes being actively involved on committees. Interviewee 4 stated that this involvement allows for relationship building in a non-selling environment and encourages trust.

Interviewee 3 recommended that firms re-evaluate how they use various activities and entertainment opportunities. You need to make sure you have a strategic reason for being involved, which could be to position yourself or your company as a thought leader.

Go/No-Go Process

Good decisions about which clients and projects to pursue have a direct correlation to your hit rate and the number of projects you are winning. Having a strong go/no-go process allows for better decision making and focused business development efforts. You have to be selective. The shotgun approach is one of desperation and will only dilute your efforts and your message. If you haven't been pre-selling and positioning yourself, you should not pursue a project.

However, recently companies have seen RFPs hitting the street before they were originally anticipated. Although the time to position themselves for this specific project was cut short, they are making better go/no-go decisions because of their relationship with the client. If they know the client, they can proceed with an appropriate response.

Many companies are also identifying their top strategic opportunities at a client level. With specific clients identified, they can focus their efforts where it makes sense, instead of responding to various opportunities as they pop up. However, they are strategic in these opportunities and have certain criteria for a client to make the list. These top pursuits allow them to stay focused and not get distracted with the random opportunities they aren't positioned for, or that don't fit into their strategy and business model.

Examples

Firm 2 is making better decisions about which projects to pursue, as well as which projects not to pursue. They have noticed an improvement in their hit rate with a strong go/no-go process review from the beginning of pursuit efforts. Their seller-doers are having the conversations across company functions, making their decisions from both operational and strategic perspectives.

While attending a recent conference, Interviewee 3 attended a session being presented by a design and construction veteran now working at a large university. The presenter reassured the audience that there is always one person's opinion that matters on a selection committee more than anyone else's. There is always a committee, but there is always one person with the power. And sometimes even the members of the selection committee don't know the true decision making dynamics. If you can address their issues, then you can win the project.

This is demonstrated by Interviewee 3 who was working with a client who was recently pursing a pediatric hospital project in the Southern United States. This firm was positioning themselves and creating relationships with who they thought that one decision maker was. They took the knowledge they gained from various conversations and translated that into their approach. They were short-listed and had a good interview. After the project was awarded to another firm, they participated in a debrief. During the debrief, they learned that the one decision maker was someone other than the person they were talking with, resulting in their approach being off from the true business problem. They learned their conversations were with all the wrong people.

As Interviewee 3 bluntly put it, "The reason the real decision-maker was so hidden is that everyone was so focused on the project delivery issues that they did not grasp the underlying strategic business issue that really drove the project into being. Had they understood that issue, they could have easily figured out who the real decision maker would be. Ironically the winning CM did not figure it out either, which is why it was an opportunity blown by the other competitors. They just happened to know the decision maker from a past project and thus became a default choice."

Seller-Doer Approach

The industry is seeing that there are fewer true business development professionals. With more companies moving toward the seller-doer approach, this decreases the sole reliance on the business development professional. Interviewee 3, however, maintains the trend toward this approach is a reactive one driven by a reduced workload, "A project executive or manager who used to be fully billable is well below the 100 percent utilization rate in many cases now with this approach. The firm will need these folks if and when they get work," he stated. "Building strategic pursuit teams involving firm leadership and 'project ops' and 'tech' with a business development in a quarterback role is proving effective."

Seemingly more companies are transitioning to the seller-doer approach, as technical and operations professionals are getting involved earlier in the game. They are realizing the benefit of a combination of efforts between a true business development professional, and the technical and operations professionals' involvement to create a better business development teaming approach. Firm 5 recently implemented a seller-doer approach and has seen a direct correlation to the increasing amount of projects won.

This strategy works because the technical and operations professionals are the ones spending the most time working directly with the clients during projects, so it's important to retain that knowledge and relationship with the client, instead of losing it as they move to the next project. Clients want to talk to the people they will be working with long before the interview and project kick-off meeting, and they want to talk to the people with technical backgrounds, not just the business development professionals.

This allows companies to create more differentiation between their firms and the competition by ultimately bringing additional value to the owners. Keeping these relationships increases hit rates for additional projects and increases the number of projects won.

Example

Interviewee 2 recently worked on an industry-wide survey on business models. The results were consistent across all A/E/C firms: they are migrating toward seller-doer models. Clients want this model and want to have conversations with the technical people they are going to be working with during the project life-cycle.

Clients are realizing that better projects result in an integrated approach with architects and contractors working together from the beginning.

Teaming

Desperate times call for desperate measures. But instead of desperation, companies are looking at teaming as an opportunity. Teaming with firms decreases the amount of competition and creates opportunities to bring dream teams together for clients. The industry is seeing big companies getting bigger. The current trend is for large companies to acquire other companies to become mega companies, resulting in a decreased number of larger firms and competition.

Likewise, integrated project delivery (IPD) is becoming a hot design approach and seems to be a common phrase. Clients are realizing that better projects result in an integrated approach with designers and contractors working together from the beginning. Construction management firms are realizing they can offer design support services. This strategy is creating better designs and more cost-effective buildings and facilities. They can help design with BIM and other modeling technology, creating an integrated approach, increasing collaboration and flexibility, while reducing inefficiencies across the board.

The IPD approach also creates an opportunity to bring a "dream team" together. With owners looking more and more at individual talent, the companies those individuals work for is less important. Bring teams together that make sense, and your individual strengths can come together to tell a compelling story and create true unique value.

Clients also want to decrease the procurement steps for any given project. An IPD contract allows them to achieve a one-step process and get everyone on board at the same time. This brings the different skills of various team players together to leverage each other's strengths.

Example

Interviewee 2 predicts that the industry will see more and more alliances. These alliances will be between organizations based on geographies or market sectors. These alliances will increase company profiles, making their differentiation hard to beat and create the ability to tell a compelling story stronger than if the companies were to pursue the work on their own. Clients are asking about individuals' talent and qualifications, not just the company's. Creating these dream teams only helps you help your clients.

Short Term Versus Permanent

All of the professionals interviewed agree the economy won't change significantly in the next ten years. This is the new normal. When the economy drastically changed in 2008, companies had to change their business development strategies and approaches to match the changing business environment. The strategies and approaches for companies now are a direct result of the changes they made. Another way to look at it is that these are changes, not reactions. And these changes are all permanent. Our new behaviors have to be long-term, or they won't be effective.

Understand Your Own Capabilities

Before you can provide your client with sound business solutions, you must understand your own company and the value you bring. You can't differentiate yourself from your competitors if you don't know what you do better than anyone else, or the true value you bring your clients. Once you know your clients' business and what they need to be successful, then you can create a specific, unique, and compelling reason for them to hire your company. You need to give them a reason to hire you and not your competition. You need to convince them your firm is the one to hire.

Example

Firm 5's main objective is to become a global organization. They want to be able to leverage client relationships outside of the United States and support their clients in every marketplace, supporting their total facility needs. Understanding what they can offer their clients will help as they become more client focused.

Cultural Changes

The only constant is change, but you have to realize you can't change your company overnight. Change takes time. As many of these national firms are making cultural changes, they are starting small and making incremental changes. They are choosing three to five initiatives and proceeding with those. Once the decisions have been made at the "C-Suite" level, they are permeating downward with the support of company leadership. These changes include the seller-doer approach, and implementing a strict go/no-go process focused on clients, not projects.

Meanwhile, many of these national firms are slow to implement changes. Interviewee 3 even indicated, "Very few firms have figured out the changes they need to make, and even those that have are struggling with them." One person described firms embracing change as "clumsy."

Trends and Considerations
Top Pursuit/Client Identification

You have to be strategic in your business development and marketing efforts. Without identifying which clients you want to work with, you will continue with the shotgun approach with little results. Keeping your company focused will pay off in the long run.

Examples

Firm 4 is currently implementing a cultural shift. They identify the top five clients for each of their market sectors, as well as a second tier of the next five clients. They are looking hard at which clients they want to continue their relationships with, and they are making the hard decision of which clients not to pursue. Once they have their top tier identified, they create strategies around each one. If something comes in the door they weren't expecting, they aren't going to pursue it. This cultural change is one that is still in the process. Not everyone was on board with this move, but as they are seeing more and more success, the leadership is buying and pushing this change down from the top.

Firm 5 has only seen success with this approach. They identified their top 100 pursuits, targeting a 45 percent win rate. To their amazement, they were able to achieve a 52 percent win rate. This drove home the idea that your goals need to parallel your strategies.

Leadership

The A/E/C leadership approach can be related to the medical profession. People don't want to walk into a doctor's office and see a doctor who is heading to retirement. They want to see a doctor just a few years out of medical school who is using state-of-the-art equipment and techniques. As in a doctor visit, our clients want to work with CMs using the latest technologies.

Clients and are getting younger, and they are having a ripple effect on how you do business. Their younger perspectives are changing how decisions are made. Most of the interviewees are also seeing clients being drawn to companies that reflect their values and culture—younger, technologically savvy, environmentally responsible, and creative problem solvers.

One critical aspect of leadership change is succession planning. Many companies' current leadership is on the verge of retirement, but these companies are realizing the next generation of company leadership isn't necessarily ready to take on that role. So the question is what to do in the meantime? They are trying to find a balance of promoting leadership from within the company, while maintaining the vision of the company.

Example

Firm 5 is in this exact situation. The current company leadership is planning for retirement. While they are committed to keeping the ownership of the company as it is currently structured, the next generation of leaders isn't ready to take over the reins. They are grooming the next generation, but they need to supplement those efforts in the meantime. They are exploring how to effectively promote from within and have a balance of new leadership, while the next generation is getting ready to take the helm.

Market Research

Before any successful business development effort can be made, you must first do your homework. You need to know your client, and more importantly, you need to know their business. Not only will this allow you to understand your client, it will give you insight to their plans for upcoming projects—both short- and long-term. While research does include website searches and other forms of general marketing research, getting your hands on real data is a must. Knowledge of financial strength, client challenges, clients' marketplace, etc., is critical for making important strategic decisions.

A common challenge for CM firms is being invited to the table early in the game. Often owners don't think they need to talk to the contractors until after the architect been selected and the design is underway.

One key to success is getting involved in the project well before the project begins, and this is best accomplished by creating relationships. Once these relationships are formed and maintained, it's much easier to be a source of solutions for the owner.

The large, national CM firms are realizing that understanding their client's business helps them provide better solutions. You need to understand how the project will impact them and add to their bottom line. This helps you to create true partnerships. It's about them making business decisions. Clients are more likely to award the project to the firm that best understands their business and will help them be more successful in their marketplace. A/E/C firms aren't the only ones in business to make a profit. Your clients want to be in business ten years down the road just like you.

Work Smarter, Not Harder
More companies are consolidating their operations and processes. They are moving toward doing things smarter, rather than harder. Some of the common approaches are implementing lean principles and making processes more efficient, which often leads to systemic changes. Many CM firms are centralizing operational tasks, which helps them to focus their efforts. Implementing lean principles and layering processes allow synergy. You don't have to recreate the wheel each time with each client and project. However, be cautious of creating a "one size fits all" approach. Centralize where it makes the best business sense without taking away from your local level focus.

Firms are also sharing institutional and project information throughout the company. Don't keep client information and success stories to yourself. Share that information with people across your company, and leverage this information and lessons learned. Realize that lessons learned in one market can help you think outside the box in other markets. Talk often so you can see trends and be able to better respond to both client and market needs.

In addition to implementing strong go/no-go processes, utilize your CRM tool manage your customer relationships. Don't start from scratch with each new pursuit. Have a centralized location for information that the entire company can access. This includes project and personnel resources, as well as trends and lessons learned. Leveraging what one part of your company has learned will help you achieve more success.

Examples
Firm 3 is in the process of centralizing certain tasks where they make the most sense. This is allowing them to have local focus, but also share project

information and lessons learned throughout the whole company, thus increasing communication and making them more efficient.

Firm 5 recently centralized all of their business development and marketing personnel into one national sales and marketing group located in their corporate headquarters. This allowed them to be more effective with their branding efforts and to create synergy and consistency across the company. Although there is one corporate department, each office that has a business development professional also has at least one marketing support person, creating a true partnering approach. This allowed them to better support company initiatives, while being able to leverage the whole company's abilities for individual projects.

Their results are an increased level of quality in their proposals and interviews, achieving synergy and consistency across the company, increasing corporate branding, and aligning business development and marketing efforts.

Technology

Technology isn't going away and owners are expecting to see it. Gone are the days of walking into a client's office with foam core boards under your arm. Many of the interviewees are seeing what used to be presented on foam core boards now being presented on iPads or other tablet devices. Client sophistication demands us to drive innovation. They are demanding the use of BIM and other 3D modeling software and solutions. There is a definite movement toward cloud based systems and having everything electronically based.

With increased client sophistication, you can't go in and just hand them a company brochure. They still want to see what you have to offer and your company information, but they want to see it presented differently using technology. They are expecting to see high-end renderings, BIM, and other 3D models.

Conclusions and Summary

Ultimately, things won't look fundamentally different in the next ten years regarding the amount of competition and how projects are awarded. Interviewee 5 referred to it as being in the second or third inning of a nine inning game. The work is out there. There will always be a need for infrastructure, and Mother Nature will always erode and damage that infrastructure, so there will always be the need for people who can put things together.

The main difference over the next decade will involve how projects are delivered. Integration is the way of the future—both with integrated design and integrated project delivery. This integration creates more flexibility and early collaboration. CMs are getting involved earlier in the game and are creating better designs. CMs are becoming design leaders, not just builders.

Most importantly, it is all about relationships. Become a solution for your clients—a problem solving resource. Help them succeed at their business. Make them realize that they need you on their team in order to be successful. Have different types of conversations with different people at all levels. Walk in telling them things they don't know. Be sure to position yourself before a specific project comes up. In your client's success, you will find your success.

6 SELLERS OF A/E/C SERVICES
Summary of Findings

Researchers/Authors: Vanessa C. Aron; Kim Icenhower, FSMPS, CPSM

Analyst/Editor: Katie van der Sleesen

Chapter 2: Sharp Shooters – Single-Discipline Prime

The primary themes uncovered during the conversations with single-discipline prime design and planning firms included the following:

- Single-discipline firms are focused on building and strengthening personal relationships with clients and partners.
- Retaining great personnel is important to the stability and longevity of client relationships.
- Understanding the client and the client's business is an important element in successful business development initiatives.
- Sellers of services must improve their ability to articulate firm and service value propositions to minimize being viewed as a commodity service that is sensitive only to price.
- Enhancing reputation and increasing visibility within the industry and with clients is a must for single-discipline firms.
- Comprehensive communications plans need to be developed that include how firms will use social media.
- Identifying future trends and being proactive and flexible in response will be important for sellers of services.

Chapter 3: Collaborators – Sub-consultants and Specialty Consultants

Sub-consultants and specialty consultants must "think like a prime professional." Firms are increasingly marketing services directly to owners and looking to gain new opportunities working under a prime contract.

When asked about future trends that may impact their businesses, most sub-consultants did not mention major industry trends like building information modeling, evidence-based design, sustainability, or integrated project delivery. Only a few interviewees mentioned one or more of these trends, though a change in the definition of "client" was mentioned by several participants. Sub-consulting firms are spending less time targeting architects and more time selling to contractors and construction managers.

What value is this information to a sub-consultant or specialty consultant? Here are a few recommended best practices:

- Think like a prime. Combine marketing efforts to A/E/C prime firms with business development also directed at owners to better position one's firm to be a member of the project team, and further direct contact with the project owner.

- Think beyond your disciplines. Be aware of trends impacting prime firms, as well as issues that impact owners. You need to speak the language of both to become a valuable member of the team.

- Train your technical staff to become better business developers. Owners are expecting technical conversations very early in the sales process, and your key technical staff have a major role to play.

- Invest in new marketing technologies, whether they relate to a more robust online presence through websites and social media, or internal software like CRM programs.

- Specialize and build your credentials for particular services or target markets. Relationships will get you part way there, but to be attractive to a prime professional, you must have the depth of experience related to the specific opportunity you are chasing.

- Diversify only in a way that makes sense for your firm. Do not abandon your core services, but find complementary services that you can offer your existing clients.

- Focus on your clients, and work to develop the business with existing accounts by providing new services or working in other client locations or facilities. Continually maintain contact with those clients that have no current work for your firm, and strive to be a source of education and knowledge to prospects, clients, and owners.

- Pay attention to major trends impacting prime professionals and contractors. If they are embracing evidence-based design, building information modeling, or integrated project delivery, chances are they will only hire sub-consultants that share their outlook.

Chapter 4: Jacks of all Trades – Multi-discipline Design and Planning

Multi-discipline firms are slowly changing the way they work. While relationships are still important, they can become a problem if you are not prepared for changes in personnel, specifically staff turnover at client and peer organizations. The multi-discipline firms who remain true to core competencies and values are finding unique ways to provide services and develop business for existing clients. The most common trend is flexibility in how and what services they provide, and to which clients.

- Thought leadership is bringing firm expertise to a client very early in the concept stage of a project to guide decisions and save design and construction time and budget. There is a growing trend to solidify relationships with current clients, as well as attract new clients, and enhance client-focused collaborations.
- Thought leadership builds brand recognition.
- Service innovation continues to distinguish firms including key hires with specialized technical expertise, exploring growing market sectors, and embracing new project delivery processes.
- Strategic teaming is an effective approach, even though firms have multiple disciplines in-house. This is due in part to changing project delivery methods. Firms must be flexible for profitable prime and sub-consultant relationships, even if that means a firm's existing service lines are not always used.
- Project managers must improve general business skills, as well as soft skills, so that long-term relationships thrive. They cannot rely solely on technical expertise.
- Gathering statistical information, measuring results, and managing data is an increasingly important business skill, and should not be foreign to A/E/C professionals.
- Project costs will continue to be a factor. Pricing work is as much about specifically defining what the client is not going to get, as it is to identify what is in the scope of work.
- Relationships may deteriorate when employees or key client contacts leave. Be prepared for personnel turnover.
- Firms that use CRM systems correctly have an advantage because they have valuable history available to technical and support staff.
- Firms not selling all disciplines are felt to be at a disadvantage.
- Retaining employees is becoming as important as retaining clients. Employees want to feel challenged by the work they do and that the projects in their firm's portfolio are a source of pride.

Chapter 5: Directors – Constructors and Construction Managers

Delivery methods, budgets, teams, and design strategies are ever-changing with the advancement of technology. In a world of adaptation, the concrete foundation to business is open communication and timeliness.

Seller: As a designer, construction manager, teammate, project outcomes and goals must be communicated throughout an entire project team. The team's internal flow of communication is critical to overall performance and project success. Understand owners' needs. Choose the proper delivery method. Assign and communicate timing of completion dates. Troubleshooting activity and costs will lead to success.

Buyer: Communication, regardless of the platform used, will be the determining factor between success and mismanaged, over-budgeted, past-deadline, project failures. Vigilance—taking a hands-on approach with a strong team—is critical. This needs to be supported by solid communication, flexibility, and openness to design modifications.

PART 2 – BUYERS OF A/E/C SERVICES

7 PREDICTABLES
Public Sector – Federal Government

Researcher/Author: Scott D. Butcher, FSMPS, CPSM

Analysts/Editors: Scott W. Braley, FAIA, FRSA; Amy Villasana-Moore, CPSM

Definition

This chapter focused on the federal government as a buyer of architectural, engineering, and construction services, with feedback from several agencies that actively engage the A/E/C community. These agencies include the Department of Veterans Affairs, U.S. Army Corps of Engineers, U.S. Department of State, U.S. General Services Administration, and U.S. Air Force, among others.

Research Design

The federal market is somewhat unique from other market sectors in that it is very rigid in its selection, contracting, and hiring practices. In many cases, selection and award is governed by laws like the Brooks Act, which mandates Qualifications-Based Selection (QBS) for professional services. While the buying behavior varies from agency to agency and contracting officer to contracting officer, the typical process is more widely recognized than with private industry. As a result, data from this chapter was gleaned from federal panel discussions at Build Business and the SMPS Maryland chapter, from presentations given at the Strategies for Success in the Federal Design and Construction Market conference, and from interviews published in SMPS Marketer.

What are your expectations of design and construction entities seeking to provide design and construction services for you?

The federal government is bound by the Brooks Act (Public Law 92-582), which was enacted in 1972 to require QBS for architectural and engineering services. This act guides the federal government's standardized process for obtaining A/E/C services. Firms interested in working on federal projects must follow this governed process to be considered.

For instance, companies must be registered in the System for Awards Management (SAM) database, which consolidates the Central Contractor Registration (CCR), Federal Agency Registration (FedReg), Online Representations and Certifications (ORCA), and Excluded Parties List System (EPLS) databases. Firms must also have a DUNS number (a nine-digit identification number for each company location), which is provided free of charge through Dun & Bradstreet.

To find project opportunities, sellers of A/E/C services must continually monitor FedBizOpps (www.fbo.gov), a website where project opportunities are posted. More than 100 federal agencies post notices for procurement of products and services to this website when the procurement value is more than $25,000. As such, FedBizOpps is a clearinghouse for federal requests for proposals.

Federal agencies have noted that the economic downturn over the past several years has spurred an increase in the number of A/E/C firms seeking opportunities to work with the federal government.

Robert L. Neary, Jr., Acting Director of the Department of Veterans Affairs' Office of Construction & Facilities in Washington, DC, noted in an SMPS Marketer interview that "We are experiencing tremendous interest in doing the work, both in the architectural design world and construction…it is a challenge. You get ten of the biggest health care delivery designers in the country and you get ten great firms. How do you decide?"

James Weller, PBS Regional Commissioner for the General Services Administration, told SMPS that firms new to federal contracting often shoot too high: "Don't just look at the big, exciting jobs; instead, look for the small, difficult jobs. Take those on and hit a home run with success in all factors: quality, price, schedule, communication. Do this and it will set you up for the larger, more glamorous jobs."

With whom do you most want to interact with when members of the design and construction industry wish to offer you their services?

While other market sectors increasingly require a technical-driven business development approach, either via seller-doers or technically-trained business development representatives, the federal government is more open to meeting with a variety of technical and non-technical professionals. However, it is increasingly difficult to gain an audience with the decision makers and decision influencers at federal agencies. It is also increasingly difficult to identify ahead of time the individuals who will be evaluating submissions. This combination makes it a challenge to determine the hot buttons most A/E/C teams strive to highlight in their submissions.

As you look ahead to the future, do you anticipate a role for non-technical marketers and business developers in seeking to provide services to you?

In general, government agencies are open to engaging both technical and non-technical business developers; it is the job of the agency to regularly meet with vendors of professional services. Often times, the contracting agents are non-technical themselves and provide a filter between the A/E/C firms and the end-users. Of all the client types, the federal government is the most open to interacting with professional sellers and marketers without technical backgrounds.

What are the most important criteria you consider when selecting a provider of design or construction services?

Most A/E/C firms working in the federal sector know that teaming is the key to success. Federal agencies have contracting requirements that dictate the target percentages of work given to small business firms of varying classifications. High emphasis is placed on a team's proven ability to meet small business utilization goals.

Most agencies have both set-aside and unrestricted procurement opportunities. The set-asides are contracts reserved for competition between firms fitting pre-defined codes including:

- Competitive 8(a)
- Emerging Small Business
- Partial Small Business
- Total Small Business
- HUBZone
- Partial Historically Black College or University (HBCU)/Minority Institution (MI)
- Total HBCU/MI
- Veteran-Owned Small Business
- Service-Disabled Veteran-Owned Small Business

As part of the rigid, prescriptive selection process for architectural and engineering services, federal agencies typically require that responding teams complete a Standard Form 330 (SF330), otherwise known as the "Architect-Engineer Qualifications." The form requires background information on the firms comprising the team, resumes of the proposed team members, relevant project examples, an experience matrix, and a free form narrative that requires respondents to address myriad issues typically published in the FedBizOpps project solicitation.

Federal Acquisition Regulation (FAR) Part 36.6 provides procedures for procuring architectural and engineering services; FAR Part 15.1 provides Source Selection Processes and Techniques to procure construction services. Although there are a number of variants of the process, a common approach for major construction contracts is the use of technical (or management) proposals and separate price proposals.

Technical proposals are typically evaluated first, followed by price proposals in order to determine the "best value" for selecting a construction firm. Indefinite Delivery Indefinite Quantity (IDIQ) contracts, Multiple Award Contracts (MAC), and Multiple Award Task Order Contracts (MATOC) are also methods by which the federal government procures design and construction services. These methods can either award contract holders directly for work over a certain time period, or can request contract holders to bid against a select group of contract holders for the work.

An alternative to the above process is the General Services Administration's (GSA) Design Excellence (and Construction Excellence) program, which entails a two-stage selection process. The first stage is heavily slanted to the lead architect (or engineer, depending upon the type of project) with their resume, portfolio, awards, and project experience holding the most importance. The lead must also typically complete a narrative regarding their proposed approach the project. Once the GSA selects the lead architect(s) with whom they intend to work, the second stage entails preparation of a more formal qualifications submission in which the entire team is presented. SMPS researchers have found that other federal agencies and entities are evolving—slowly and deliberately—to experimentation with and acceptance of the two-step process.

For construction firms, FAR 28.102 requires that all construction projects of $100,000 or greater be subject to the Miller Act. This means that performance and payment bonds are required; typically 100 percent of the original contract price plus 100 percent of any price increases.

Past performance is also a critical component of selection. Every federal contract holder receives a performance rating at varying stages of their contract. A procuring agency will review these ratings during the selection process and will contact the references provided in the submission. Firms with poor marks will likely be eliminated. Firms with little or no federal project experience must find ways to prove their performance capabilities under federal procurement policies.

What are the most effective approaches to offering design and construction services to you?

Most federal agencies actually serve as brokers; they are responsible for a number of districts, divisions, installations, or other missions. While the agency manages procurement and contracting, often the end-user is more amenable to meeting with a proactive A/E/C representative, which can provide firms the opportunity to acquire a more thorough understanding of a given project's issues.

Firms and teams must respect the "code of silence" that surrounds a project once the solicitation is posted. Meetings and interactions with federal representatives related to a specific project are typically not allowed after advertisement.

In general, agency representatives appreciate a firm who approaches a meeting prepared with ideas that can help the agency achieve a current goal. Firms are advised to present new technologies, innovative approaches, or proven solutions to similar challenges.

Due to the prescriptive nature of federal submissions, it is extremely important to ensure that A/E/C sellers not take liberties with the proposal requirements. Firms that do not follow the submission requirements as outlined in the FedBizOpps procurement solicitation risk immediate disqualification without ever having their submission reviewed by the selection committee.

As mentioned previously, teaming is often a critical component in working with the federal government. The various agencies have goals for small business and small disadvantaged businesses, either as direct prime professionals, or as part of a subcontracting plan. As a result, the subcontracting plan is an important component of the selection process and A/E/C firms must have teams in place to meet this requirement. Teams experienced at working together typically score higher than ad-hoc teams pulled together for a specific project pursuit. Teaming arrangements can be prime contractor/subcontractor(s) or can take the form of a joint venture.

Mentor-protégé relationships are also encouraged by federal agencies. This program of the Small Business Administration (SBA) entails an approval process for mentors, who in turn provide assistance to 8(a) firms that are part of the program. In theory and in most cases, these relationships benefit both the mentor and protégé. However, in practicality and real life, some relationships live up to the hype and expectations while others fall short. The key to success lies in the motives of individual firms and their willingness to collaborate in an open manner. Technically, the mentor-protégé relationships must last at least one year. However, in many cases these firms tend to stay connected for an extended period of time once a relationship is established and is working well.

Interestingly, some agencies have open door policies for business developers to meet with contracting officers, while others limit the access to their contracting staff because of workload requirements, coupled with the overwhelming number of A/E/C firms attempting to call on them. Some agencies recommend meeting and interacting with their staff through organizations like the Society of American Military Engineers (SAME), or at panel discussions for professional and technical organizations.

What are the least effective approaches to offering design and construction services to you?

With so many firms pursuing federal government opportunities, contracting officers are faced with the challenge of filtering through dozens of submissions for certain projects. On the design-side, this often means evaluating SF330 packages, first for submissions that do NOT meet the requirements outlined in the project solicitation. Many SF330 packages have lengthy lists of issues and instructions—sometimes down to the number of pages, required font, and minimum point size. If the solicitation states that the SF330 should be in Times New Roman with a font size of at least eleven point, a firm submitting an otherwise perfect SF330 in Arial ten point can be eliminated before their hard work is ever reviewed.

Not conforming to the RFP requirements is the easiest way to narrow the pool of candidates for a project. As a GSA representative stated at an SMPS Build Business program: "It's not how great your package is; it's what's in the package. If the RFP says something, be sure to check it off because we're looking at ways to eliminate you."

In the rush to pursue projects, firms often do not make the best go/no-go decisions, thus limiting their ability to succeed within the Federal market. The SF330 provides a built-in tool for this. Section E of the form requests the resumes of key personnel assigned to the team, while Section F allows for up to ten example projects to demonstrate the respondent's qualifications. Section G, "Key Personnel Participation in Example Projects," overlays the two previous sections to demonstrate that the staff listed in Section E worked on the projects listed in Section F. Agency representatives recommend that firms review this matrix with a critical eye. If the key staff members have not worked on at least some of the example projects together, the team will most likely not be considered highly qualified. Conversely, if the team provides projects that no one on the proposed team has worked on, those projects will not be reviewed.

Because so many firms with no previous federal experience are chasing projects, most are finding themselves frustrated due to their lack of success.

A representative from the GSA told an SMPS audience to "Start small, forget the home run…get your foot in the door, and become a proven commodity."

For firms that do not get selected for a contract, it is recommended that they request a debriefing from the contracting officer. This process allows firms to gain a better understanding of what they did correctly and where their submission fell short. This process also provides vital feedback to assist A/E/C firms with the evaluation of future opportunities and the genesis of submittals for them. The agency often publishes guidelines regarding when and how to request a debriefing. The debriefing will only cover the strengths and weaknesses of the team's submission, not how it compared to other teams.

As you look forward to the next ten years, what trends and considerations will most influence how you purchase design and construction services?

Several trends have emerged in recent years, and they show signs of increasing in the decade to come.

The most obvious trend is the movement toward sustainability, which for some agencies means requiring the U.S. Green Building Council's Leadership in Energy and Environmental Design (LEED) program's LEED Certification.

In 2006, nineteen federal agencies committed to guiding principles for sustainability. Over the next few years Executive Order 13423, Executive Order 13514, and the Energy Independence and Security Act of 2007 (EISA) further advanced sustainability through mandates for reduced energy and water use, while setting the stage for high performance government buildings.

The GSA, for example, has embraced LEED. In 2012 and 2013, the Green Building Advisory Committee of the GSA evaluated 160 green building rating tools and opted to stay with LEED for GSA buildings because it best met the requirements of the EISA. After initially adopting LEED Silver as the certification standard for new construction and substantial renovation of federally-owned buildings, the GSA increased the minimum requirement to LEED Gold.

The next major sustainability initiatives within federal agencies are buildings with: Net Zero Energy use on an annual basis; implementation of renewable energy strategies like solar and geothermal; and more aggressive uses of energy conservation strategies. Agencies are increasingly looking at total ownership costs: design costs, construction costs, and life-cycle costs.

Many agencies have moved toward awarding much of their architecture, engineering, and construction work through term contracts that are known variably as Multiple Award Contracts (MAC), Multiple Award Task Order

Contracts (MATOC), or Indefinite Delivery Indefinite Quantity contracts (IDIQ). Under this contracting approach, agencies can select a pool of design and construction firms and award them individual task orders, instead of advertising for each project separately. When several firms are awarded contracts (as few as two and as many as seven), the agency identifies those MAC or MATOC contract holders that are best suited to the task order scope at hand, and then makes their selection based upon brief submittals that address approach, experience, and competitive pricing.

Funding and budgetary changes during the fiscal year often affect an agency's ability to advance projects. Agencies may use funded contract vehicles to help other agencies achieve their goals. MAC, MATOC, or IDIQ contract holders may find themselves under consideration for projects with an agency other than the agency holding their contract. Similarly, agencies are more open to variations on the public-private partnership model to fill funding gaps, although this approach takes both creativity and leadership approval.

Project delivery is changing significantly as many agencies have moved toward design-build as a preferred contracting approach over design-bid-build. In fact, more than 70 percent of the Department of Defense's A/E/C projects are now procured via the design-build methods. While other agencies have not yet reached this level, most understand the value of early contractor involvement on a project and have taken steps to ensure that contractors start providing input during a project's design stage.

Building Information Modeling (BIM) has become a standard within many federal agencies. This has created a competitive advantage for those firms with a deep resume of BIM experience, putting those design and construction firms that do not have the requisite experience at a disadvantage. BIM is changing within federal agencies as well, as the end-users are looking for ways to evolve the Building Information Model into a facilities management tool. Also, BIM is a component of another trend within the federal sector: lean construction. Approaching the construction process in a way more akin to manufacturing, lean construction entails prefabrication and modularization of a building's components offsite, thus reducing project schedules, while enhancing quality and helping with construction site safety.

Throughout the past decade, overseas work has largely been focused on the Middle East, particularly Iraq and Afghanistan. Federal agencies that operate internationally, like the Department of Defense, are looking toward the Pacific Rim for increased activity over the next decade. The U.S. Department of State also offers international opportunities for A/E/C firms through the Bureau of Overseas Buildings Operations. The U.S. Agency for International Development (USAID) is also active in procurement.

Aging building stock is a major issue for federal buildings and the agencies that operate them. For instance, the Department of Veterans Affairs owns more than fifty-five hundred buildings and leases an additional sixteen hundred, covering more than 142 million square feet. The average age of these buildings is approaching sixty years.

The Department of Veterans Affairs is faced with a continual challenge to modernize its facilities, while balancing very real budgetary constraints. Because of this, operations and maintenance programs will be robust in the coming years.

Conclusions and Summary

Unlike private market sectors, federal buyers are bound by law to procure architectural, engineering, and construction services in a prescriptive process. The Federal Acquisition Regulation (FAR) outlines the process for selecting firms and teams, and laws like the Brooks Act and the Miller Act mandate qualifications-based selection for A/E/C services, and performance and payment bonds for construction projects greater than $100,000 respectively.

Sellers of A/E/C services must strive to forge relationships with contracting officers at federal agencies, though their ability to access these individuals has become increasingly difficult in recent years. For non-technical business developers, the federal market is one in which they can successfully operate, as they are often developing relationships with contracting officers who are often non-technical and thus do not expect to have technical conversations.

While relationships are key factors, qualifications are extremely important and conformance to project solicitation requirements is vital. Firms that do not meet the minimum contract qualifications or requirements will often not make it through the first round of elimination, despite favorable relationships with the contracting officers and end-users. Due to the volume of submissions received for design and construction procurement, firms are often eliminated because they did not follow the solicitation announcement or RFP exactly as required.

Trends in federal government design and construction mirror those in other market sectors. Sustainability is not a new trend, although the requirements for sustainable buildings have been increasing since passage of EISA in 2007. Beyond LEED certification, agencies are now looking toward Net Zero Energy buildings and renewable energy sources as the federal government continues to be a mainstay in environmental stewardship.

Many agencies now require BIM, consequently creating a gap between those design and construction firms with a deep resume of BIM projects and those with little or no experience. Firms with limited BIM track records may find themselves increasingly unable to meet the minimum qualifications for projects.

International opportunities will continue, with agencies like the Department of Defense looking increasingly toward Pacific Rim projects in the coming decade.

The age of federal building stock is a major issue, and building modernizations, as well as operations and maintenance projects, will be emphasized throughout the next decade. This trend will marry with the BIM trend as end-users begin integrating Building Information Models into their life-cycle management process.

8 DEPENDABLES
Public Sector – State, County, Municipal

Researchers/Authors: Taree Bollinger, CPSM; Mary Beth Perring, FSMPS

Analysts/Editors: Adam Kilbourne, CPSM; Fawn Radmanich, CPSM

Definition

This chapter deals with public agency owners, including: state government bodies, counties, municipalities, special purpose districts, ports, and authorities. The size of the state and local public sector market suggests continued opportunities for enterprising marketers both in the short- and long-term. Given the magnitude of the current public infrastructure market, publicly run institutions, such as universities or hospitals, are treated in a separate chapter. The 2012 Census Report tallied 89,004 local governments including 3,031 counties, 19,522 municipalities, 16,364 townships, 37,203 special districts, and 12,884 independent school districts. These figures do not even include states and state agencies.

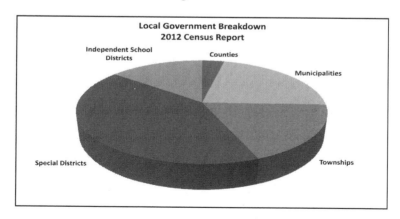

Research Design

The information provided in this chapter was gathered from in-person and telephone interviews with those on the front lines: the public officials and staff representing agencies throughout the nation. Each individual was asked six baseline questions. The information shared with us was cross-referenced with media reports and other published materials.

What are your expectations of design and construction entities seeking to provide design and construction to you?

Nearly all of the state and local clients we interviewed stressed the importance of relationship-building. The hierarchical structure of public agencies means firms must build multiple relationships up, down, and across client organizations, as well as be able to discern what role each has in the decision-making process.

Across the board, we heard from our interviewees that state and local agencies are looking for firms who understand their needs, offer solutions that save money or add value, and demonstrate a track-record of delivering quality projects in such a way that makes their lives, and their staff's jobs, easier.

"Cities are obligated to put work out to bid," said Marilynne Beard, Deputy City Manager of Kirkland, Washington. "But I want to know that you have done your homework, that you know my community and my organization and what is unique about us. I can spot boilerplate a mile away."

Others echoed her sentiments.

"I think business developers would do well to remember that clients do business with people they like and that your word is your bond," said Marnie Primmer, Executive Director of Mobility 21, the Southern California Transportation Coalition. "When you're building a relationship with a client, you need to be consistent, you need to make sure you're there for them even when the money isn't, and you need to make sure you do what you say you're going to do. When their budgets expand, if they have measures on the front and you're there, they will remember that."

It is critical to get to know the managers and establish ongoing relationships with key decision-makers if you want to capture a share of the direct award market. This is true whether you work in a state such as Washington where state agencies, municipalities, and special purpose districts are allowed to bypass the RFP process and award work under certain dollar limits directly IF the contracting firm is listed on the city/district roster, or with agencies where the acceptance of federal funds dictates an RFP process. An increasing level of turnover of public officials, discussed later in this chapter, however, is making this more challenging in some cases.

With whom do you most want to interact when members of the design and construction industry wish to offer you their services (e.g., principal, senior executive, project manager, technical staff, marketer, business development representative, etc.)?

Quite simply, it depends on who you talk to. Public clients generally have multiple levels of decision makers and influencers. Different levels have different interests, which determines who they want to talk to.

Decision makers who have technical backgrounds and technical responsibility for projects made it clear they want to talk to the "doers." They want to know what sort of technical ideas and solutions you can bring to the table, and they want to make sure they have confidence and trust in the consultants they will be relying on.

On the other hand, if the ultimate decision-maker is an elected official, they are more interested in talking to senior management or non-technical business developers who can explain technical concepts in a way they understand. Better yet is someone who is knowledgeable of funding opportunities and processes, or who can explain how their approach to a project will generate public support—including at the polls.

"I feel very strongly about hiring design and construction firms with a focus on sustainable outputs and firms that have the team-building as well as the technical skills to assist with public outreach, finance, permitting, construction inspection, and start-up, and will follow through oversight during the warranty period." said Larry Haag, former Mayor of Washington, Indiana.

Mobility 21's Primmer acknowledges that the answer is not a simple one.

"I think this is a conundrum that many business developers face, because there are doer-sellers, and they're few and far between, and they're worth their weight in gold," she said. "But for the most part business developers are not technical experts, and technical experts don't have the communication skills necessary for doing that relationship building. So I wouldn't say it's an either/or process."

The type of person clients want to interact with can also depend on where you are in the sales cycle. One mayor from a small midwestern town with a technical background put it this way: initially he's fine with non-technical people calling on him to learn what the community needs and how their firm can help, but as specific projects develop, he wants to talk to the project manager and designer. Then at some point in the first six months, he wants to hear from senior management to show that the firm values his business and is committed to him as a client.

As you look to the future, is there a role for non-technical marketers and business developers in seeking to provide services to you?

Simply put, state and municipal clients are most interested in whoever can help them. If a non-technical business developer can advocate for funding, facilitate collaboration between agencies to help a project happen, or garner needed support for a project (i.e., from elected officials, regulatory agencies, and stakeholders), they will be welcomed.

According to Haag, "Marketers will need to become more involved at all levels of the project process…conception through final project completion. They will need to become more hands on and engaged with public involvement."

Beard encourages marketers to understand and explain how they will help city staff and officials to address the gamut of issues that cities have to consider when investing in capital improvements: Is it green? How can we extend the life span? How can we make it more cost effective?

"If you don't want the hassle, don't bid on it. It's not for the faint of heart," Beard advises. "Ultimately, which projects get funded is a result of public policy and political will to achieve public good," she added.

Since support of a non-technical variety is becoming more and more important to agencies, the role of marketers could grow. In fact, the director of procurement at a state department of transportation noted that while their managers and staff want to meet with technical professionals, he saw a role for non-technical marketing staff, even in project meetings "because they listen better."

However, if non-technical marketers don't understand what they are selling or can't bring value to the conversation, then clients saw it as an annoying waste of their increasingly limited time and resources.

What are the most important criteria you consider when selecting a provider of design or construction services?

Every client wants to feel like they are your "No. 1" client, that they can trust you to deliver projects successfully, and that you will communicate with them throughout the project.

Alex Greenwood, Planning & Economic Development Manager at the City of Brentwood, California said, "The things that matter to me are: have I worked with the company before or do I have people I respect who have worked with the company before? How has the track record been in terms of project management, of providing design services that help in the overall objective of delivering a high quality project that is on time and on budget?"

Beyond the project itself, agencies are also looking for A/E/C firms to act as advocates for funding and legislation.

"My expectation is that engineering and design companies that do business in the transportation market will be engaged from an advocacy standpoint to make sure that the industry is taken care of, and that they will work together across modes and across service lines within their own companies to get projects built efficiently for the public," Primmer shared.

To raise needed infrastructure funds, agencies and elected officials must convince taxpayers of the need to foot some very large bills. These taxpayers are going through their own belt-tightening and are becoming more vocal in their displeasure about anything they suspect may be wasteful spending. Agencies are looking to A/E/C firms for help. Enterprising A/E/C firms may find they can increase their market share if they can help agencies educate community members and stakeholders on the rationale behind capital improvements and the consequences of not investing in them.

Clients across the board are also looking for innovative ways to stretch their funds and consultants who can offer new approaches.

"We are challenging designers to be more innovative," said Louis Feagans, Project Management Manager, for the Indiana Department of Transportation. "We need more practical design solutions that help us leverage our funding. We also want consultants to help us prioritize the 'fixes.'"

As a counter point, Beard cautions that tight resources are creating a risk-averse environment where defaulting to proven technologies is the often the safest route. "The latest and the greatest may not be the right way to go when you are under the microscope of public scrutiny," she warns.

The economics of construction and life-cycle costs are also receiving more attention these days. For example, Chip Comilla, Director of Public Works in Bradford, Pennsylvania, noted that when tackling new projects A/E/C firms "need to show proven pay-back in life-cycle costs within a few years not spread out over fifteen or thirty years."

This attention to costs may also mean consultants will need to propose phasing or other solutions that gets the ball rolling now, even when the entire project cost isn't available. "Some projects will need to be phased and may take a lot longer to get built. I think that the community dynamics will continue to be very challenging; we are looking at a very complicated political situation," said Greenwood.

What are the most effective and least effective approaches to offer design and construction services to you?

Most public agency leaders interviewed were very direct on this point:

- Be friendly.
- Be respectful of our time.
- Bring something to the table—don't just expect to get work.
- Be truthful whenever an issue arises.

Among the least-effective approaches mentioned were firms who brought their top project manager to the interview, then switched to someone less experienced or capable once the contract was in place.

As Don Eng, retired Chief Engineer, City of San Francisco Department of Public Works, put it, "Often the firm brings Burt Reynolds to the interview, then puts Pee Wee Herman on the project."

Other pet peeves included talking down to them; talking more about themselves than the client's needs; and proposing unrealistic solutions.

As you look forward to the next ten years, what trends and considerations will most influence how you purchase design and construction services?

While state and local clients want many of the same things that other clients do, they told us that they face very different and increasingly complex pressures than those in the private sector—pressures that firms must remain keenly attuned to when marketing to this sector.

The Big Squeeze

The challenge is not whether there will be work to be done, but how state agencies, cities, special purpose districts, and other local governmental bodies will fund the enormous cost of rebuilding our nation's roads, bridges, sewer/water pipelines, power grids, treatment plants, dams, and other major infrastructure, while simultaneously dealing with the political realities that will accompany such a massive outlay. Cuts in federal and state funding to communities, declining tax revenues, and increasing regulatory requirements have had a drastic and nationwide impact on this market sector from 2008 to 2013 These trends are expected to continue.

- America has a backlog of infrastructure projects valued at over $2 trillion to be completed over the next five years [by 2014] according to a report issued by the American Society of Civil Engineers (ASCE) in 2009.[1]

- In their 2013 Report Card, the ASCE concluded that to get our infrastructure to an acceptable level, a total investment of $3.6 trillion is needed by 2020.[2]

- All states are facing the enormity of the financial crises: Maryland $100 million a year to fix bridges; Virginia $125 million a year to repave crumbling roads; the District of Columbia $806 million to replace a rusting bridge.[3]

---

[1] American Society of Civil Engineers, *2009 Report Card for America's Infrastructure*, 2009, 2.

[2] Doug Scott, "ASCE's New Report Card Bumps the Nation's Infrastructure Grade Up to a D+," *ASCE News*, March 2013, http://www.asce.org/ascenews/search.aspx (accessed 29 Mar 2013).

[3] *Burden for Rebuilding Infrastructure May Fall to States, by Ashley Halsey III, The Washington Post,* 27 October 2012.

- In fiscal year 2010, local governments lost 2.6 percent of their state aid and 2.5 percent of their property tax revenues from the previous year, for a total of $25 billion. The two revenue sources had not declined simultaneously since 1980."[4]

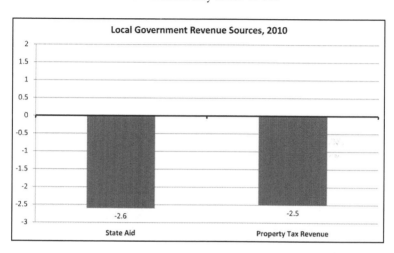

Tackling the need to address the nation's crumbling infrastructure and finding the funding sources to do it will remain the major concern and likely be the driver of any changes. Despite these needs, most of the public sector owners interviewed did not anticipate major changes to the procurement process because it is largely governed by federal and state laws attached to funding. Any major changes to procurement would be legislative and most clients didn't anticipate that happening anytime soon.

"The average person thinks that 'money just appears' in city management," Beard said. "They are not aware of the public financing mechanisms that are in place. There is no free lunch and never has been and never will be."

Many sector leaders don't anticipate any substantial increase in funding soon either.

"The federal gas tax hasn't been raised in twenty years, and frankly may not be the best source for long-term transportation funding," Primmer said. "What do we need to fund our infrastructure? There's a huge shortfall annually between the level of funding needed to maintain and expand our system and what the gas tax generates, what the need is and what the assessment is, and at some point that's going to catch up with us."

And these leaders expect consultants to be on the frontlines of these discussions with public officials. Feagens believes that the need for more

---

[4] The Pew Charitable Trust, *The Local Squeeze, Falling Revenues and Growing Demands for Service Challenge Cities, Counties and School Districts, American Cities Project*, 1 June 2012, 3.

funding, and educating the public on why funding is needed, is a long-term trend. He added that the problems the public sector is facing are becoming more and more complex, as well as more and more costly. "In 2002, the state [Indiana] needed $500 million just for preservation: in today's dollars that equates to $780 million," he said. "At the same time, for every mile that average fuel efficiency improves, the state loses $20 million in revenues."

Then there's the increasingly complex regulatory environment public agencies must deal with. "Politicians are always adding rules, but rarely do they take them away," Beard said. "Cities understand that they don't always get the cheapest work. There are layers of accountability and rules."

"Rules mean reporting is required," she adds "We don't always like the rules. I appreciate a private entity showing respect for and understanding of the rules we [city managers] all have to abide by."

Public Projects Under the Microscope

The transparency provided by the Internet and the 24/7 news cycle is increasing the level of scrutiny projects invite, be it from stakeholders, citizens, or media who now have a variety of public channels to air their concerns and complaints. While these concerns may be expressed by those who possess little technical understanding, elected and appointed officials increasingly find themselves on the spot, needing to explain complex technical and regulatory issues.

Even after a project is approved, the public's desire for transparency in government is making the decisions and actions of elected and public officials increasingly open to scrutiny and criticism. The result is that elected officials, subject to pressure from local constituencies, are becoming less tolerant of changes in scopes once projects begin, regardless of the reason.

"The days of bidding low and asking for change orders are waning," Beard said. "It is harder for cities to obtain additional project funding even if conditions change as a project unfolds. Public agencies expect contractors to do their homework before they bid on the project. Furthermore, as stated earlier, public sector clients are asking for 'no-risk' guarantees, or at least agreements that are very low risk to them."

A public works director for a medium-sized, midwestern city, who asked not to be named, confided, "Many public officials have elevated [their] expectations of performance to the extent it is becoming more common for public officials to expect design professionals to produce near perfect products. This is evident in both public and private contracts in which clients request or demand contract terms that establish unreasonably high standards and require any deficiencies be corrected at no cost to the public."

He believes this situation will indirectly impact those marketing to the public sector and explained that this trend of expecting near perfect or perfect projects makes public staff officials seem unreasonable to deal with at times compared to their private counterparts. Even though the public officials have consideration for unforeseen circumstances within the design or construction life of a project, they do not want to answer to their bosses, the elected officials, who have taken on a more aggressive mindset toward public employees, their performance, and the selection of consultants. This may result in the cost of projects going up, not down.

"Design and construction services will either need more contingencies built into the public official's budget, or design and construction fees will continue to increase beyond the normal growth of annual costs of materials and labor," he explains. "As a public official, I would accept above normal growth of annual costs of materials and labor if it meant I would not have to request additional funding from the board of aldermen or city council. In other words, the way elected officials act these days, I would rather have the city pay more up front, than have elected officials make determinations throughout the life of the contract resulting from any possible changes."

The result is public managers cannot afford to make a mistake or hire a contractor who can't get the job done. Those marketing in this arena must be able to sell the "abilities" of their firm: deliver-ability, financial st-ability, product reli-ability, and staffing depend-ability.

As an aside, the impact of increased transparency is also spilling over to the procurement process. For example, a few years ago the Indiana Department of Transportation began publishing all proposals submitted for projects to its website, along with scoring documents. This allows savvy firms to compare their proposals and scores with those of their competitors, keeping the bar moving higher and higher. One department of transportation manager explained how he liked to compare proposals from competing firms electronically using two screens and key word searches.

Putting All of the Puzzle Pieces Together

One way interviewees told us they are overcoming funding challenges is by becoming more collaborative and establishing public-private and public-public partnerships.

For example, in 2012, the citizens of Sammamish, Washington voted to contribute $25 million in construction funding in a joint project with the YMCA to build a 60,000 square-foot community center that would include a pool and water park. The city provided the site. The YMCA will contribute $5 million toward the construction of the facility and $1 million for equipment and furnishings. Once built, the city will own the facility, but the YMCA will operate it and assume the ongoing profit or loss.

Comilla shared that his department is currently funding some of its parks projects through private donations.

And Greenwood said, "If twenty government agencies need to partner to make a project happen, and if there are ten different funding sources (local, state, and federal), and if the project needs to be phased over time, then those are all factors that design professionals need to be savvy about and adjust their tactics accordingly."

These partnerships also add a new wrinkle to the design and construction process. Greenwood pointed out that while public-public partnerships often spread out the cost of a project over a number of agencies, they also add a layer of political complexity. Consultants need to balance the agendas of different client agencies, for example, automobiles versus transit.

As mentioned at the outset, selling to public sector clients has always involved multiple decision-makers and influencers at many levels. Now marketers must also develop relationships with their public and private partners, and sort through all of the layers to determine where the real authority for decision-making rests.

Marketers who position themselves to broker, or at least foster, collaboration, however, will benefit.

According to Primmer, "From a standpoint of market forces acting on the infrastructure market, I would say that ability to use public-private partnerships to augment the funding that is not coming from the federal and state governments, coupled with the ability to do local funding measures, is the kind of future I see for transportation funding."

Public Workforce in Transition

Also complicating the relationship-building process is an increasing rate of turnover of public officials—both elected officials and agencies leaders. This means that relationships are not as long-lasting as they used to be and that business developers may be marketing to several generations. A principal for FCS GROUP shared that while her list of agency clients has changed little, more than half of her contacts at those agencies have left in the last year. Others have also noted the trend.

Pew Charitable Trust reports that "through a combination of layoffs, attrition, hiring freezes, and furloughs, local governments shed half a million jobs, or 3.4 percent of their overall workforce between September 2008 and December 2011 with half of this loss coming from the education sector. At the same time, states eliminated an additional 150,000 jobs, or about 2.9 percent of their workers. And these jobs are not expected to come back any time soon."[4]

"I see this as a cyclical shift occurring, as opposed to the loss of more tenured public officials, because of the recent economy in the last four years," said Scott Smith, former Public Works Director for the City of

---

[4] The Pew Charitable Trusts, *The Local Squeeze*, 13.

Wentzville, Missouri. "However, I am not sure how long this trend will continue."

Turnover is also a side effect of the political process that shapes city management and has always been an issue for the public sector. "The average job span for a city manager is only five to seven years. They [city managers] serve at the pleasure of the city council. When a new council comes in on a platform of change, they change what is visible—city management," Beard stated.

The aging workforce and the incumbent turnover holds a hidden benefit for some firms marketing to the public sector, however. It opens the door for consultants to fill the talent gap, either through public-private partnerships, or serving as an extension of staff and temporarily filling the vacancies with staff from within consultant firms.

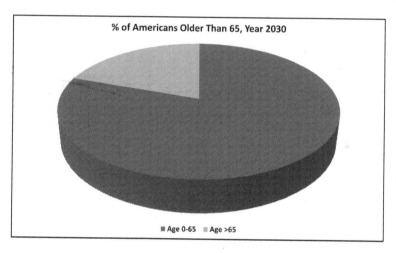

According to the Washington City Manager Association's New Generation website (www.wccma.org/newgen.htm), "The maturing of America will have a direct impact on the social, physical, and focal fabric of our nation and its communities. By 2030, the number of Americans over the age of sixty-five is projected to be 71.5 million—or one in five people. More significantly, 44 percent of local government managers are fifty-one years or older and will retire within the decade." This is further explained by the ICMA Next Generation Initiatives, "A much smaller group of young and career changing professionals are in line and prepared to fill their shoes. There just aren't enough people."[5]. With a growing number of near-term retirements and too few younger generation professionals in the work force, agencies' abilities to staff projects are diminishing.

---

[5] International City/County Management Association (ICMA), "What Are ICMA's Next Generation Initiatives?," http://icma.org/en/icma/priorities/next_generation, (accessed 01 Apr 2013).

The Future of Local Government

While there is clearly a large backlog of public work, we would be remiss not to point out the increasing number of news reports on city and agency bankruptcy filings. According to the authors of an article published in the Los Angeles Times, the decision by three California cities (Stockton, Mammoth Lakes, and San Bernardino) to seek bankruptcy protection in the space of two weeks in 2012 "underscores the mounting financial pressure facing local governments around the country. Collapsing property values and entrenched unemployment have pushed cities and counties to the economic brink. Tax receipts in some locales have shrunk more than 20 percent over the last three years, and soaring pension costs exceed funding levels by as much as $3 trillion nationwide."[6]

The bankruptcy trend is not limited to California, nor to cities; Jefferson County, Alabama, recently became the largest agency to file for Chapter 9 protection in U.S. history. The Los Angeles Times article also points out that in "Michigan, four cities and three school districts are currently operating under emergency management by the state, which means the local officials have effectively lost their administrative power. Three other cities in the state, including Detroit, are operating under consent agreements that may end in having their finances taken over as well. The City of Scranton, Pennsylvania, the article continues, cut all municipal pay to just $7.25— minimum wage. The mayor has proposed an 80 percent increase in property taxes to help close a nearly $17 million budget deficit, a move that could help Scranton stave off bankruptcy."

Across the nation in communities of all sizes, from mayors to state agency directors to public works superintendents, our interviewees confirmed the concerns voiced herein are very real and the solutions still unclear, particularly given the complexities of operating in the public arena.

Conclusions and Summary

Public sector agencies differ from private sector businesses in that they are highly regulated and procedure-driven; they are also beholden to their constituents—especially at the local level. While they have access to a mix of tax revenues, grants, user fees, and revenue bonds that are not as available to the private sector, these funding sources are not always reliable.

Much of our public infrastructure is reaching the limits of its useful lifespan and needs to be renovated or replaced. As cited earlier, some sources estimate our current infrastructure backlog could be as high as $3.6 trillion, but at the same time, funding sources for rebuilding the

---

6 Ken Bensinger, Kim Christensen and Jessica Garrison, Los Angeles Times, "Bankruptcy choices highlight fiscal pain of cities nationwide," 15 July 2012.

infrastructure are on the decline. As a result, few would argue that current financial pressures are merely part of a cyclical pattern. The magnitude of the challenge is beyond what we have experienced in years.

Public agencies are also increasingly dealing with climate conditions that exacerbate the need to replace infrastructure earlier than planned and straining already tight budgets. Major events such as Hurricane Katrina, Superstorm Sandy, and severe flooding followed by drought throughout the midwest in recent years, are especially ominous because such disasters are always non-discriminatory. Natural disasters don't distinguish between aging and new infrastructure.

"Of the $60 billion requested by the Obama Administration in emergency supplemental funds for recovery efforts for Hurricane Sandy, $12 billion would be earmarked for the U.S. Department of Transportation, largely for restoration of damaged transit systems." [7]

In short, it is not a case of if, but how soon, with what, and by whom, our aging infrastructure will be replaced. Mushrooming costs are forcing agencies to find new solutions that look and feel decidedly different from the infrastructure used by previous generations.

Meeting these challenges under increasing regulatory burdens, political pressures from constituents is affecting not only how public sector infrastructure projects are being procured, but the structure of the public agencies themselves. We predict that when it comes to state and local public sector business development, we will be dealing with a "different animal" for the foreseeable future.

Large, small, or mid-sized, none of the agencies caught in the epicenter of this storm are immune. The key to marketing successfully to the future state and local public sector might well be in the A/E/C industry's ability to understand this new reality and for business developers to adopt a new mantra: "A problem cannot be solved by the same level of thinking that created it," [8] a quote often attributed to Albert Einstein.

Regardless of who originally said it, it sums up this chapter quite nicely: those business developers who are able to offer uncommon solutions will likely gain, or maintain, the largest market share in the evolving public sector arena now and over the next five to ten years.

---

[7] American Council of Engineering Companies, "White House Requests $60.4 Billion for Hurricane Sandy Recovery; $12 Billion for Transit Repair," *The Last Word*, 12 December 2012.
[8] http://Thinkexist.com.

9 ENTREPRENEURS
Corporate, Commercial, Hospitality

Researchers/Authors: Dennis Paoletti, FSMPS, FAIA, FASA; Jeffrey Taub, CPSM; Joy L. Woo, CPSM, LEED AP

Analyst/Editor: Janet E. Brooks, CPSM

Definition

This chapter focuses on business development trends as viewed by owners in the corporate, commercial, and hospitality sectors of the architecture, engineering, and construction industries.

Research Design

The findings and trends presented in this chapter are based on primary research: interviews conducted directly with key representatives responsible for selecting consultants for design, construction, or both assignments within these sectors. The research team established a standard set of questions that would serve as the basis for determining trends in these sectors. If the interviewee agreed to an interview, the interviewer used the questions as a guide, but was not required to ask every question and could ask other follow-up questions depending on how the interview proceeded. The questions were asked by telephone or email, depending on the respondent's preference.

Of the twenty-four owner representatives interviewed, the majority (eighteen or 75 percent) are in the commercial sector with the remainder in the corporate or hospitality sectors. The roles of these sector representatives include presidents, executive and senior vice presidents of development, senior project managers, and real estate directors. Companies represented include, among others, Equity One, Fortuna, Hines, Liberty Property Trust, MGM Resorts International, Related Companies, Thor Equities, Silvercup Studios, Google, and the New York Jets.

Situational Analysis

The research team found no significant distinctions in findings and trends across the corporate, commercial, and hospitality sectors to indicate they have meaningful differences in their consideration of existing and future business development practices.

Research Findings

Existing Business Development Environment

Business development practices continue to be relevant to most owners, but it is important to understand how a particular owner prefers to be engaged. Most preferred working with firms that they have worked with in the past. "Our best outreach is through people we already know," stated John Madeo, Executive Vice President of Mountco Construction and Development Corp. However, some owners will meet with new firms as a courtesy to learn more about them, particularly if introduced or referred by someone they know and trust because there is a mutual understanding of integrity and reputation at stake.

As emphasized by one real estate executive, "I usually get in touch with firms by word of mouth, but do entertain business presentations every once in a while. We have picked up some new vendors both ways, but word of mouth has been more successful."

Local presence, both in the community and at industry events and conferences, also plays a role. We work with most of our local design and construction firms," said Michael Printup, President of Watkins Glen International. "We are always networking for future clients and relationships, so our paths cross often in the community."

The table below lists some of the likes and dislikes of the owners who were interviewed.

BD Activities: Likes and Dislikes

Likes
Specific and formal presentations with pitches tailored to owners' projects or needs
Lunch and learns are valuable
Occasional calls from people they know about important changes that impact our work or relationship (staff changes, promotions, new expertise, high-profile assignments)
Seeing the team in their office
Industry organizations for networking

Industry-wide events
Collaboration on new opportunity
Introduction to new clients
Dislikes
Cold calls without pertinent information
Pitches to the wrong audience
General presentations: nothing specific to owners' needs or wrong audience and expectation
Meet and greets
Being wined and dined
Events put on by an individual firm
Time-consuming activities: general socializing with firms who want to do business with the owner's company

Some owners are interested in getting to know their consultants both in and out of the office to build mutual trust. "Any time that you can share time with long-time and potentially new firms and contacts outside of the typical business environment having discussions both industry-related and on a personal level, I feel is a good thing," stated one industry executive.

In general, everyone is busy and owners want their time to be respected; firms seeking to engage owners must do the research and make their information relevant and specific.

As noted by Steven Goldin, former Chairman and CEO of InterCap Holdings, "I believe in the rifle approach—be specific in presenting me with the skills or services I need now. It is a poor reflection on the company if they don't do their homework first and approach me with services that I don't need."

Said another real estate executive, "I am not a huge fan of certain business development practices, but I recognize that they are part of how our industry does business. Often, I just don't have time to listen to pitches, particularly if they're not relevant to anything I'm working on." Some owners will socialize in a number of ways with the team once they are all selected and working on a project together.

Owners offered some interesting advice. Many noted that a firm's website is a critical resource for owners as they research firms and learn about their capabilities at their own leisure. Among our respondents, social media is not viewed as a critical or useful business development tool at this time, nor in the near future. Also, tried and true reputation building activities such as maintaining a presence at trade shows and exposure as a result of writing papers and giving presentations are beneficial to expanding one's reputation. This can be costly and may be a questionable use of a firm's time and money. Each firm must carefully evaluate the potential benefits and return on investment for participating in trade shows.

Finding the Decision Makers

Owners in these sectors make purchasing decisions in a variety of ways. Although a few noted group decision making, the majority of final decisions are made by a senior member of the organization, whether they hold the title of chief executive officer, president, executive vice president, senior vice president, vice president, partner, director, project manager, or leader.

A few owners make recommendations to their clients, who in turn, make the ultimate decision. According to a senior vice president of a global real estate services firm, decision making may vary by project and client. In this case, project managers or the client may make the decision, or a joint decision between the project manager and client is made.

In at least one case, the owner's internal architectural and engineering team chose the consultant.

From these responses, a basic tenet of business development must continue to be followed: cover all bases and make every effort to identify and convince the ultimate decision maker and influencers along the way.

How the Decision Is Made

Determining factors and selection criteria include many of the basics that have been applied in the design and construction industry for years. Owners who were interviewed noted the importance of these factors and criteria listed in random order below.

Determining Factors/Selection Criteria

Reputation/word of mouth
Highly competent, highly professional people and firms
Staffing/experience of team members proposed/capability
Chemistry between consultant and owner teams
Easy to work with
Can-do attitude/go above and beyond
Best overall proposal, not just cost
Project history and relevant experience/track record
References
Area of expertise
Local knowledge
Quality of design, work, product/smart design
Problem-solving ability/creativity
Sustainability/"green" focus
Accessibility
Relationship with consultant/track record working with owner
Response time/meeting deadlines
Price/cost

Owners do not see these factors and criteria changing, and the marketing industry has been well aware of the importance of many of these basic selection criteria for quite some time. A vice president at a hospitality firm noted that service both during and after the project is completed is an important factor. This implies that it is not only important to build and maintain your reputation during a project, but well after the project, so you will be considered for future opportunities. "Past performance with happy and satisfied clients will bring repeat business. Once a client is happy with the performance, they will come back to you even if you are not the lowest bidder," stated Kishor Joshi, Vice President of Sheena, Inc.

The importance of references was a recurring theme among respondents. As one executive stated, "I rarely use new firms unless I have references or recommendations about them from other firms that I trust."

The corporate, commercial, and hospitality sectors are comprised of a competitive, but tightly-knit group of owners, and reputations spread fast. "Reputation is key," said Mary Byrne, Senior Vice President of ividence, inc. "A referral from a trusted industry colleague would be a big driver in choosing the right firm."

The Role of Non-Technical Business Developers

Of the owners interviewed, 80 percent do not see a role for non-technical or junior business developers, especially if they are not key members of the project team. Our respondents prefer to meet with principals, senior technical staff, the project director, and people who would be working on their assignments. They want to talk to the designer, engineer, or scientist, for example, who is enthusiastic about his or her work and believes in what he or she does.

As stated by Jerry Lea, Senior Vice President, Conceptual Construction, Hines, international real estate firm, "[We are] not interested in talking to business development-only folks. We want to meet and talk with the key project director who will be responsible for our project."

The belief that sales pitches are wasted on seasoned veterans of the design and construction industry was pervasive among the respondents.

A senior vice president from a prominent commercial real estate owner and developer also prefers to interact with people that do the work. "I would much rather talk to an engineer who is thirty years into his or her career and is now focusing on new business generation, promoting his or her firm, and knowing the business thoroughly, rather than a person hired solely for new business that has never actually executed a project," she said.

"I am wowed by the solid business expertise and the enthusiasm and energy behind someone who believes in what they do." The same executive finds some business development people are more successful at getting their message out than others. "I think it's a tough job and takes just the right personality," she said, and "I think it is essential that they know their business well and convey that enthusiastically."

If the business developer has a technical background and works on projects, however, there may be a role for him or her. For the 20 percent of owners in the minority, the business developer could play a role in establishing rapport with owners by doing basic preliminary research or sharing information about a firm's changes (recent promotions or new staff announcements keep owners abreast of talent). They must, however, have a thorough understanding of the type of work and project being considered.

> "There is no role for non-technical business developers in our market because we seek design and construction support for specific project needs, such as opening or renovating an office," said Steve Schlesinger, CEO of Schlesinger Associates. "We don't seek non-project-specific pitches from design and construction firms. We really want to communicate with the technical professionals who will be working on our projects."

"A business developer who really understands what he is selling can be effective," stated Steven Goldin, former Chairman and CEO, InterCap Holdings. This sentiment is echoed by a real estate investment executive, who also sees a role for business developers provided that they understand the technical nature of their services. "If the business development people understand the work and the jobs, there is a place for them," he stated. "There is not if they are simply salesmen."

Differences Among Design and Construction Firms

Owners, for the most part, view design and construction firms differently. Some of those differences are illustrated in the table below.

Architects/Designers	Construction Firms/Contractors
Softer; specific skills	More clear cut; physical ability
Expertise on specific project	Means and methods
Know the locale and codes and regulations	Familiarity with building type and size
Good design/innovation	Relationship with subcontractors
Good coordinated set of construction documents	Logistics capabilities; adequate manpower to complete the assignment

Although differences are viewed, the trend is toward a graying of lines between designers and contractors; as noted by a director of real estate, "Design firms are moving toward looking like contractors and contractors are moving more toward looking like design firms."

One real estate executive noted that "because architecture and engineering are so specialized and different from one another, we will trend toward a collaborative approach utilizing more than one firm."

The differences among A/E/C firms and their business development practices will likely influence the structure of successful proposers and bidders in the future. Some architectural firms are learning how to think and act like contractors, and vice versa. They are attempting to learn how to collaborate together to meet the single point of contact criteria that some owners are looking for.

Regardless of the differences, the same basic factors and criteria noted previously are still desired, most notably: reputation, relevant experience, and references.

Is Location a Factor?

The location of a firm plays an important role in the future of business development. With the ability to market from afar using web-based conferencing, smartphones, mobile apps, social media, and high-powered video technology, relationships can be cultivated and maintained from farther away than ever before. What may be lost in social proximity can be gained in the efficiencies of time and space.

Responses to firm location varied considerably among owners interviewed. Some prefer to work with local firms that know the local market, economy, and players, whenever possible. This is especially true of contractors. Some owners state that location is not as important as it used to be; one global resort owner notes that they use firms from all over the world, especially, high-end architectural designers. Some owners distinguish proximity based on project size.

For example, a vice president of design and development noted, "Location is important for smaller projects. It is not at all important for larger, complex international projects." Still others see location as less important than responsiveness and ability to meet deadlines.

Owners continue to see face-to-face meetings as critical in project success and required to produce results, especially for site visits and walk-throughs, controlled inspections, and seeing eye-to-eye. They see some utility to virtual meetings depending on the situation, but they do not see them as a complete replacement for in-person meetings. As stated by Stuart

Rubinfeld, President of Matel Realty, "I see virtual tours and 3D visualization playing a more prominent role in the future, but they will never fully replace the real thing. There is a tactile element to a real estate project that requires a physical interaction." One real estate executive agrees: "I do not like virtual firms; I like to meet people in person and look them in the eye and make sure they are crystal clear on the work required."

The Role of Technology

Most owners stated that firms should be leading-edge. "I expect more online capacity and speed to increase, even more information to be moved via central file systems, and for BIM to become more widely used and accepted," stated Mark Gold, Director of Real Estate for Silvercup Studios. Several owners note that BIM is important as it continues to grow in prominence, and other technologies mentioned included Revit, 3D modeling, and visual simulations. Regardless of their technical background, business developers will need to speak intelligently on the changing nature of project delivery tools and technologies.

Avi Kollenscher, Vice President of The Related Companies, noted that "the digital landscape is changing and cutting-edge firms will do better with us than firms that cannot adapt. We have been presented with cutting-edge solutions recently by a consultant."

Business development will help inform the project delivery practices of owners in the commercial, corporate, and hospitality markets. "Technology will continue to grow and impact the profession; the ability of professionals to grow with the technology will be important," stated a director of real estate and design and construction.

Owners are typically not driving new business development technologies or innovation. It is the A/E/C firms that bring new technologies to the marketplace, the interviews, and the projects. They are the ones "ahead of the curve" in their efforts to establish themselves as unique in their field and in their attempt to be selected for a new project. From there, others (i.e., competitors) follow and catch-up. Owners initially select based on uniqueness, then come to expect the new approach, technique, or solution as commonplace and expect the same service, process, and technique from the rest of the industry.

A wide variety of project delivery methods are currently available, and new methods of working continue to be developed. Project type and size seems to be a key factor in determining which project delivery method and owner prefers.

Design-build, especially on simple projects and projects with repetitive features, can be a successful delivery method, although one owner does not embrace design-build or integrated project delivery noting that the owner loses control, especially in a fixed-fee contract.

For most owners, public-private partnerships are definitely a trend, especially as the risk is shared, which is more appealing. "Change is good, especially in means and methods. Change is also dependent on economic background. The greater the risk and less available capital, the more change and experimentation there will be," noted Thad Sheely, Executive Vice President of Stadium Development + Finance for the New York Jets during design and construction of the new MetLife Stadium.

A commercial property manager pointed out that business developers could be helpful in establishing relationships with real estate developers on the type of work they represent. "A thorough understanding of new construction and development methods they are using to streamline or advance the productivity of construction projects," he stated, "would be an advantage in bidding to secure work. Regardless of methods or techniques, many owners view collaboration and shared values among the team and between the consultant and the owner as critical.

Application of technology is important to owners as long as the basics are covered. Stuart Rubinfeld, President of Matel Realty, shared some ideas on the effects of technology in the next ten years: "I can pre-qualify a firm through online research before the in-person pitch. Use of tablets to show ideas and portfolios at a trade show is revolutionary versus building and staffing costly and time-consuming booths. Virtual tours and digital visualization can better mimic sunlight, shadows, and other physical considerations, and virtual tours can even show how a room or building changes hour to hour (whereas models are static and cumbersome). I am interested to see how 3D technology in movies can be used by design and construction firms in their business development efforts."

Architectural, engineering, and construction firms need to at least stay current with technology. Being a leader and staying a step ahead of the competition is extremely important in today's marketplace, regardless of what industry is being considered. Any firm that is technologically challenged would be of concern.

"It's important to stay on the cutting edge of the latest trends and technologies to help potentially reduce costs," noted Jeffrey Yachmetz, Director of Development for Thor Equities.

Moreover, firms should bring new technology to owners, not the reverse. Steve Schlesinger, CEO of Schlesinger Associates, sees first-hand the role technology is already playing in the business development process. "We're not bringing new technological ideas to our architects in their line of work, so that's coming from them," he said. "We're seeing documents and samples a lot faster than before, and seeing three-dimensional views of our prospective space as opposed to simple renderings."

It is all about prioritizing client service. "I can tell you that any tool that makes the process easier for the client is key," stated Mary Byrne.

What does the mergers and acquisitions trend mean for business developers?

Successful design and construction firms will continue to understand and deliver results to address owner needs. The basics of Marketing 101—know to whom you are selling and how to meet their needs—will not change. Firms must continue to find ways to differentiate themselves. Collaboration and integrating sustainability into design are also important.

The majority of respondents do not see full-service firms as the answer to their problems or projects. They want the best people for the job and if they must bring together the best from several firms, they will. These owners recognize that quantity does not imply quality—and many are "nervous" about or "suspicious" of full-service firms, as they cannot be the best at everything.

> "Successful design and construction firms will be the ones who have the best people; that is the most important factor," said a real estate development executive. "I don't see any real benefit, either in terms of coordination or pricing, from using one large, full-service firm."

Karen Backus, President of K. Backus & Associates, recognizes that the quality of individual people trumps the depth of full-service firms. "I like to assemble teams so I know the client is getting the best of each specialty."

Just as one of the basic marketing premises is to know to whom one is selling, it behooves each A/E/C firm to fully understand their strengths and weaknesses in delivering services.

One commercial property developer took the onus on himself to make a multi-firm team work.

"I want the very best people and firms working on my projects, and I'm willing to go through the extra management time to make it happen," he said. "I will go to larger firms with integrated services for their horsepower and will pay the premium—not necessarily for their expertise, but for their ability to turn work around quickly. But I will never compromise by hiring a less talented or skilled individual or firm for the sake of expediency or management time. I want the very best at each position."

Some owners believe that a single, multi-disciplinary firm is fine because of efficiencies that are possible for small projects, but for larger projects, more research is done to find the most appropriate firms and they are likely to utilize individual firms with specific recognized skills, individuals, or reputation that are not available within a single firm.

Ross Asseltine, Senior Project Manager in the real estate industry, stated, "In the past [before the digital age], single full-service firms were beneficial.

Now, we would rather pick the selected individuals from any firms who have the talent and reputation to best serve our project and not be tied to a single firm for all services."

Others, like David Duvoisin, an Associate of the Fortuna Realty Group, see one firm as the future trend. "I think the future is a 'one-stop-shop' design and construction firm that has all or most of the necessary capabilities in house for ease of coordination and productivity."

Regardless of the single-service or full-service nature of a firm, some respondents circled back to the basics: work hard, communicate, maintain integrity, and utilize technology. As stated by a real estate executive, "I think firms that stay current in their work, and a step ahead in their technology, with good old-fashioned values will succeed. I think firms that fall short in their ethics, communications, collaboration, professionalism, and technology, will fall behind."

Conclusions and Summary

Owners in these sectors are not interested in non-technical business developers; they want to meet the actual architects, engineers, and builders to select the best firm for their job. They also want respect for their time, and advise that only pertinent project and industry-related information is presented to them. Sharing news about a firm's high-profile projects, recent promotions, or new key staff are welcomed by most owners. In-person meetings remain invaluable in promoting trust through social interaction.

Design and construction firms should maintain their industry visibility at trade shows, industry events, and the like, but reputation, referral, and word-of-mouth are essential to success. Relative to selection, most owners want the best people for their projects—regardless of whether they work for a full-service or specialized firm. Stability and loyalty is important.

Design and construction firms must embrace new technology—particularly when it comes to external communications and business development—to brand themselves as progressive and capable of meeting technological challenges. Owners depend on design and construction firms to develop new and beneficial means and methods to employ their services using the most advanced technologies for the benefit of the owners.

10 SYSTEMS
Educational, Health Care, Institutional

Researchers/Authors: Cindy Jackson, FSMPS, CPSM;
Craig Park, FSMPS, Assoc. AIA; Steve Ryherd, CPSM, LEED AP
Analysts/Editors: Janet E. Brooks, CPSM; Fawn Radmanich, CPSM

Definition
This chapter looks at public sector client perspectives, including design and building professionals from client organizations that included higher education, health care, publically-funded institutions, and non-profit charitable organizations. These organizations all share fiscal responsibility to public shareholders and boards, and generally approach A/E/C selection through an open-advertisement request for qualifications (RFQ) process.

Research Design
Our contributors represent a cross-section of public sector clients including: Jay Bond, AIA, Associate Vice President, California State University, Fullerton, CA; Arthur Deist, Senior Program Manager, Biomedical Safety & Facilities Engineering, American Red Cross, Pittsburgh, PA; Marshall Ellis, Director, Real Estate Management, American Red Cross, Charlotte, NC; Kim Fender, Public Library of Cincinnati and Hamilton County, Cincinnati, OH; Dr. Edward Hughes, President/CEO, Gateway Community & Technical College, Covington, KY; Stanley Horrell, Director, Campus Planning & Sustainability, Metropolitan Community College, Omaha, NE; George Killian, University Facilities Management Professional; Mary Beth McGrew, AIA, University Architect & Associate Vice President, University of Cincinnati, Cincinnati, OH; Pete Midden, FCH, Director of Facilities Management, Fleming County Hospital, Flemingsburg, KY; Jason Taylor, Project Manager,

American Red Cross, Charlotte, NC; and, Howard Wertheimer, AIA, LEED AP, Georgia Institute of Technology, Atlanta, GA.

Each of these client representatives interact directly with A/E/C firms at the marketing and technical level, and through one-on-one interviews, shared their views on how their organizations interact with business developers and marketers from those firms.

In our interviews with facility professionals from a variety of public institutions, we discussed their perspective on expectations of quality of service, preferences for points of contact, the role of the non-technical marketers and business developers, key selection criteria, effective (or ineffective) marketing and business development tactics, and the future trends they see in the procurement of professional services.

We found their responses to these overarching questions to be consistent and provide excellent guidance to the A/E/C business developer in how to build a successful relationship with a public non-profit institution regardless of their focus.

What are your expectations of design and construction entities seeking to provide design and construction to you?

To be successful with institutional clients in the next decade, the A/E/C business development professional will need to demonstrate foresight in navigating rapidly shifting organizational forms that are themselves adapting to more limited resources and increasing demands for higher quality service.[9]

Jay Bond, Associate Vice President for Facilities Planning & Management/Campus Architect, California State University, Fullerton, noted, "In the last few years, we've seen a significant reduction in capital spending. Because of that, attitudes change. While we remain positive, we are not building the big projects we were just a few years ago. I trust that will come around. I think demand will return in the end. These issues are scary, but I believe we will get through it."

Bond added, "When the marketing professional is knowledgeable, they can demonstrate sincerity in meeting our needs rather than only in meeting *their* needs. It can be subtle, but there are people who come in the door

---

[9] Wilen-Daugenti, Dr. Tracey, Vice President & Managing Director, Apollo Research Institute. Retrieved from keynote presentation at SCUP North Central Conference, University of Illinois, Champaign-Urbana, November 2012.

looking for work, and then there are those who come in the door looking to be of service. When it is more about us than it is about them, we listen."

A/E/C firms will increasingly be called upon to assemble inter-disciplinary resources that their clients and potential clients will need and expect. To be successful, they will need to be more adaptive to cross-discipline collaboration and less focused on the role of "sole practitioner" or "prime consultant."

Howard Wertheimer, Architect and Director of Capital Planning & Space Management at the Georgia Institute of Technology, emphasized this issue stating, "Being a state university, we need to have local participation. Local firms are learning how to seek out experts if they don't have that expertise…and those partnerships will continue to evolve." Mr. Wertheimer, however, is adamant in pointing out, "Firms have pictures and people have experience. The resumes that are in the proposal as part of the team had better align with the photographs."

George Killian, who works in facilities management with a large midwestern university, said, "I see a future of blended skills. I see the business developer of the future having more technical expertise, and technical people with more marketing skills."

Keys to meeting this changing landscape will include developing the ability to:

- Analyze vast amounts of data and to understand data based reasoning.
- Assess and develop positioning content that uses new media forms and leverages these for persuasive communication.
- Work productively and demonstrate presence as a member of a virtual team.

The Internet—massive, open, and ubiquitous—has given public sector clients unparalleled access to comparative and competitive insight into the expertise, experience, and quality of the work product of professional service firms.

Dr. Edward Hughes, CEO of Gateway Community & Technical College, said, "I expect them to listen to what we need first, and then respond to that with their expertise, and then enter into a dialogue about how we arrive at the final plan. I've been around a long time and worked with a lot of A/E/C firms. I've had the contractor from hell and I've had the architect from hell and in both cases the primary issue was they didn't listen. They didn't respond to what we were saying. Perhaps, they thought it was my fault because I didn't articulate it or because I didn't know their language. The firm's representative, whether technical or non-technical, needs to help me understand the language or a least help me translate."

Arthur Deist, Project Manager, Safety & Facilities Engineering, American Red Cross, added, "Today, we are so busy, that more often than not, we might make the first contact with an A/E/C firm. We do reference checking and online research. You can tell a lot about a firm from their website."

Pete Midden, Director of Facilities of Fleming County Hospital, noted, "Design professionals need to listen to their clients very closely and don't just assume something is going to happen or not going to happen. When you're designing a hospital, you are looking into the future. The A/E/C firms we work with need to think about what I am going to be doing five years or ten years from now in the hospital. We actually look a little bit further down the line than that. Sometimes A/E/C firms overlook that and only look at where we are today."

Skills for the 21st Century

Public institutions—education at the primary, secondary, and post-secondary levels; health care providers at the local and regional community level; and non-profit capital campaign and volunteer giving based institutions—are largely the products of an organizational and structural infrastructure and societal circumstances of the past.

Understanding that from the client's perspective their economic landscape has changed, these institutions are now learning how to adapt quickly. Responding to this change will be critical to the success of the A/E/C business developer. New skills those changes require include:

- Developing critical thinking, insight, and analysis capabilities.
- Integrating new media literacy into marketing programs.
- Developing the ability to collaborate, work in groups, read social cues, and respond adaptively.
- Integrating interdisciplinary thinking into the team structure that incorporates a broad range of skills and knowledge on a broad range of subjects.

Quality Service

In every case, those interviewed emphasized that they have a high expectation for expert knowledge, quality delivery (e.g., on time, on budget, and few, if any, change orders), strong communication skills, and reliability as the "cost of entry" to do business with them. We in the industry hear this every day, but it seems—based on the client's interactions—that few A/E/C service providers actually live up to their own hype.

Stanley Horrell said, "One of the most important things that any firm can bring is a solution that fits the scale of this institution, but also respects the culture of our college. That's a challenge, but important."

Killian added, "Focus on the customer. Listening and understanding what the customer really needs is critical. Another important differentiator for firms is bringing relevant research or evidenced-base design to our projects."

Marshall Ellis, Director, Real Estate Management, American Red Cross said, "The American Red Cross is a bit different than many public or non-profit organizations. Where a local education or health care institution may do a few projects each year, the Red Cross owns or leases more than 13 million square feet of space spread over more than eighteen hundred locations (eleven hundred leased, seven hundred owned). As a result, it often has more than one hundred projects a year."

CSU Fullerton's Bond added, "We have the luxury as a large institutional client that people want to serve us. We have high expectations, but we also have no lack of design, engineering, or construction talent in the region. We have some of the best and brightest, so competition is intense."

Mary Beth McGrew, University Architect, University of Cincinnati, said, "The A/E/C firm needs to be an extension of our staff. Whether it is to do planning, design, or construction, there has to be constant communication and conversation. The more we can clearly define what we need, and the consultant can carefully ask us questions, the easier it becomes. I know when it doesn't happen; we all pay for it dearly."

Howard Wertheimer agreed, stating, "We have a remarkable pool of qualified people…We are fortunate to attract good, quality consultants who are interested in pursuing work at Georgia Tech and we try to treat them fairly…and have a functional, beautiful building at the end of the day. We want everything in the right place and it has to work."

Kim Fender, Director of the Public Library of Cincinnati and Hamilton County, noted, "Our expectations are that the service provider would fully understand exactly what we are doing and why. As laymen, we do not always have the best understanding of what the architects and engineers can do." She was critical about a key issue, saying, "One of the most frustrating things working with them as an owner is that they rarely understand deadlines. We have a very fixed schedule and because of state law, we have certain steps we have to go through before we can do work. If we miss one of those deadlines, it can postpone the work by months. So meeting those deadlines is absolutely crucial for us. At the end of the day, we have to feel confident that they are going to do what we expect them to do."

For each of these public sector client types, the A/E/C professional interacts with two different tiers of clients. First, there are those in the facilities entity (directors, project managers, and facilities and maintenance staff) that represent those who have experience with design, engineering, and construction, and have often been putting buildings together throughout their careers. The other tier is the functional client (academic, physician, and administrative staff) who may not have a deep understanding of the design and construction industry and have probably not built anything at the scale the facilities group typically sees.

Bond added, "For the user it's a once in a lifetime experience. We play the part of a buffer. It's hard for the uninitiated client to understand that construction is difficult, that design isn't always flawless, and that people can make mistakes, forget things, and be misinterpreted. Our expectations are high and we are demanding in that regard. Because of the depth of resources available to us, we have the ability to build relationships so that architects and engineers get to know each other over time."

Marshall Ellis, Red Cross, said, "The Red Cross is a lot like other large institutions. We have a 'supply chain management' team, where A/E/C firms can register into our database. While A/E/C firms generally don't like to do that because it offers little in the way to differentiate, the odds of making the cold call at the right time for a project are slim."

Ellis noted that two primary service groups of the Red Cross include: Humanitarian Services that focuses on local community needs and disaster relief, and Biomedical Services that manages national blood collection and distribution. Where its local and regional Humanitarian Services offices are much more like typical office buildings, the Red Cross' blood facilities—because of the regulatory issues governing its use—are more akin to a pharmaceutical organization, with FDA and other agency standards and reviews, commissioning and validating processes, and with more stringent technical requirements.

"It is important for the professional service firm to understand these differences," Ellis added.

Deist, Red Cross, noted, "Even though we are a non-profit entity, we still need to go through full design, building codes review, and construction administration. From our view, non-profit is no different from for-profit. We are required to be competitive. Every few years we solicit qualifications for task order contracts, selecting a group of A/E/C providers, so that when projects come through we can negotiate based on predetermined fees, change order rates, overhead, etc. We still obtain competitive bids for this work, but from this pre-selected list."

Jason Taylor, Project Manager, Real Estate Management, Red Cross, added, "We try to use this task order process where we can, but we also do a lot of small turnkey projects, acting more like a general contractor, because the work is primarily tenant improvement ranging from HVAC to furniture procurement. As such, at times we work with smaller, more local firms, who come to us through referrals from the landlord or other tenants."

University of Cincinnati's McGrew, commented, "I can't expect the A/E/C firm to know everything we know or talk to everybody that we talk to on campus. I expect the consultant to expose me to something I may not have considered. So I look for people who offer considerations of something new."

With whom do you most want to interact when members of the design and construction industry wish to offer you their services (e.g., principal, senior executive, project manager, technical staff, marketer, business development representative, etc.)?

In each case, those interviewed stated that clearly understanding their organization—their structure, history, economic, and political environment—before contacting them, or anyone in their institution, was the most important factor to a successful first introduction. Simply making an appointment to talk about your firm, your history, and your portfolio of experience was of little or no value, and, in fact, may be counterproductive.

Gateway Community College's Hughes, said, "I want to see the decision maker at the right level for the right decision. I don't want to have to go to the senior principal for something that somebody else on the team can handle. That doesn't make any sense to me. I want to see the person who I'm going to look across the table to and be held accountable."

Jason Taylor, Red Cross, said, "Because my projects are small, marketing to me is not necessarily the highest priority. I am more than happy to talk to anyone from the business, but the firm needs to be visible within the community. Where a firm might be represented on one of our Red Cross chapter boards, they become a source for referrals, but for projects within the chapter, it must be recused from participating in the work."

George Killian added, "The right point of contact is different for different stages of a project. I don't mind seeing the business developer at the beginning of the process, to get to know the firm. However, the qualifications of your project manager will be important. There will always be personality differences. Firms need to understand that the people skills of their project managers and technical staff are as important as those of the business developer. If they don't have good interaction and communications skills, they can really damage our professional relationship."

Fleming County Hospital's Midden, said, "I want to talk with the project manager. Usually the principals have a hand in what's going on, but the project manager is the one I see on a regular basis. That's who I need to interact with. This would be the same for new facilities, expansions, and renovations because they are actually the people putting it on the paper and actually putting it together. And we need to be on the same page all the time."

Metro Community College's Horrell commented, "I think the marketing or business development representative often does a better job at first contact. Because in that meeting it's about sales; business developers often have a more comfortable, easier way of engaging. They are used to working with a wide group of people and don't come off as overly technical. It's not like they are bringing a specific point of view, but more that of a generalist. Once they understand the scope and scale, they may bring a more technical person."

Georgia Tech's Wertheimer was once a seller-doer at an architecture firm in Atlanta and appreciates the business development process. "I always appreciated the time that people gave me throughout my career, and I try to reciprocate because I know how meaningful it was to me," he said. In addition, Wertheimer acknowledged, "Every client organization is different. Every representative of that organization is different." He added, "You want to be as broad and deep as you possibly can."

Mary Beth McGrew, said, "I need to meet the people who are the leaders of the firm because they set the tone for the firm, and when the project gets going, the technical people are most helpful. It's different in different phases of the project. At the interviews, I need to feel a bond that I can work with that person. For the project to be successful, I need to be able to face this person through disagreements—the joys and sorrows of any job that runs its course. During the technical stages, I want the first class geeks."

Taylor, Red Cross, said, "There is no perfect time, but I'm always willing to sit down and meet. I think the best approach is to show that you spent the time to really understand the Red Cross needs and goals. Perfunctory visits are less important. With limited funds, we are much more tactical in how we procure services for our capital projects. There is little chance that a cold call would come at the right time to position for a project."

Cincinnati Library's Fender, noted, "We would certainly expect the person we meet with to fully understand our project needs. We would expect them to have enough knowledge to be able to explain the project. I know some people only want to deal with principals, but I don't have an issue with that. I do think it has to be somebody who can answer questions and who has the authority to speak for the design firm."

As you look to the future, is there a role for non-technical marketers and business developers in seeking to provide services to you?

The client's perspective on the role of the non-technical marketing and business developer was mixed. Many view them as an important step in getting to know a firm, but several we interviewed did not see them as a serious participant except as providers of general information, as compared to licensed or practice-side building industry professionals.

Deist, Red Cross, said, "In my opinion, the only role a non-technical person can fill is to help put together proposals, or other back-end functions. If you don't have technical expertise, it is not a beneficial business development position to assist the Red Cross."

CSU Fullerton's Bond gave an alternate view, saying, "Initial outreach is typically by the marketing professional. The marketer will set up a time for me to meet their leadership and that's when I get to meet the principals and senior executives. I don't mind the marketer being there. They can be really helpful, but I prefer not to meet them alone."

Bond added, "The most important element for marketing to us is that the A/E/C firm needs to know something about us before contacting us. That is an important role that the marketing professional can play. The principals and technical staff rarely have the time or energy to really do that well, but when done well, when the marketing comes in knowledgeable, it can demonstrate more sincerity in meeting our needs than in meeting only their needs."

University Architect, Mary Beth McGrew, said, "I think there's a role for non-technical marketers. You always have to have people that write clearly, that write well. I don't think you can depend on your people who are designing systems or designing buildings to be able to tell the story of your firm's brand. When I open the submittal that you send and I read the cover letter, it sets the tone for the proposal. I don't flip to the pictures. I want to read what you say to me. Is it a stock letter or do I have someone who I know who is talking to me. I think there is a role. You need someone to say 'I hear you and understand you.' You can't underestimate the value of thinking critically. As I go through the submission, if I can find the answers and they make it painless for me to read, it does make a difference."

Metro CC's Horrell said, "In a lot of long-term successful firms, the principal has done business development for years. However, that can be a problem. Often when the job is started, the principal disappears and the troops do the work. That feels like bait and switch. Principals should be at meetings throughout the course of the project."

Gateway College's Hughes added, "During one selection process, one of the key players on the team we selected was a non-technical person. I thought she added tremendous value to their team. She wasn't technical, she wasn't an architect, but she knew the language and she knew education so she could bridge that language when we didn't understand a concept."

George Killian said, "I find that networking in the community is an important way to meet the people who know people you need to know."

Library Director Fender agreed, saying, "While we may not have defined a specific project that requires technical expertise, if we sat down and talked with someone about the overall services the firm could provide, that might just be something that I was struggling with."

Georgia Tech's Wertheimer sees the value in non-technical business developers noting, "It is nice to have relationships with those business development folks, but the business development person isn't going to be the person sitting around a table working on a project together. They are the 'relationship manager,' 'bridge-builder,' 'liaison'—but they don't have the subject matter expertise that will add value to whatever the project opportunity is."

In Wertheimer's view, effective business developers have been smart people who knew enough to be able to carry on an intelligent conversation, but also knew the importance of saying, 'I would like to introduce you to one of the partners of the firm, or this project manager, or this design person, who I think you'd enjoy meeting.'

Pete Midden, added, "There is a place for the non-technical marketer. In the beginning of a project, working together, we can often come up with good ideas and then turn it over to the architects and engineers."

What are the most important criteria you consider when selecting a provider of design or construction services?

"Understand my institution, before you call me!" was the consistent and oft-repeated refrain from every person interviewed. Based on their experience, too often that understanding came 'on the job' and not before, which led to a learning curve much greater than necessary and a post-project value perception much lower than possible.

Metro CC's Horrell said, "It is critical that you understand our mission and culture and be able to convey that understanding. Too many firms come to the interview only touting their past accomplishments, not realizing that they wouldn't be in the interview if we didn't already understand that they were capable of doing the work. We don't need a rehash of your past accomplishments. We need a demonstration of genuine interest and an understanding of what our project is and that you bring the right team to the interview, I mean the people who will actually do the work, not just a group of 'suits' that will not actually work on the project."

120

Fleming Hospital's Midden agreed, saying, "Listen to your client. When it comes to selection of A/E/C firms, everybody has an expertise. You could build the best building in the world, but if it's not what the client needs, it's worthless."

George Killian noted, "Match your firm's qualifications to the job at hand. Architects tend to say they are everything to everybody, but often don't have any real experience for a particular project. My job is to understand what their skill sets really are so they can be successful, and our clients get the project they want. At the end of the day, it is the people that do the work. Those relationships are critical to our selection process. If an individual leaves a firm, it will take a while for us to get as comfortable with their replacement."

Killian's experience with some institutions sees the selection process changing. He noted that a number have gone away from the typical 30-minute presentation (e.g., PowerPoint, models, display boards, and printed leave-behinds) and now focus more on team dynamics. Instead, after the traditional long-list, short-list RFQ process, these institutions specify who they want to be at the interview, and do not allow them to bring any presentation materials. Teams are tasked with answering a series of multi-part questions in one hour—questions they have not heard before they enter the room. The selection is based on not only how those questions are answered, but how the team interacts in delivering their response.

Killian added, "Before we implemented this process, we would get people in an interview that we never would see again. A project is like getting a new job. You have to sell yourself to the committee on your communication skills. You would not be sitting here if you weren't qualified. By making the short list we don't need to see qualifications again. We want to see your response to real life situations we find on a project," said Killian.

She continued, "I think taking this approach has been a big plus—a move in the right direction. There are firms that struggle with this process, but most have appreciated the benefit of really being able to present their team's communication capabilities. When you are going to be with someone for three to four years, the last thing we want is to work with someone we will continually butt heads with."

Cincinnati Library's Kim Fender, added, "First, is the firm qualified to do the work that we're looking for? Next, have we worked with them before? If we haven't worked with them before, have they worked with another library or another public entity before? Finally, have they done public bidding in Ohio before? Our state regulations can be a challenge. We want those basic qualifications, then relevant project experience and public bid experience if at all possible. We need somebody who really has an in-depth knowledge."

Georgia Tech has a multi-phased process like most other institutions, but emphasizes specificity of individual team members and project experience. "We realize at any point in time that people may change around," Wertheimer said. He noted that he also wants to see some resumes and not just a firm name and perceptions of their qualifications in the marketplace. As for project experience, it is important to Wertheimer to have specific experience in higher education.

"If it's a laboratory facility we are looking for, I don't need to know they worked on student housing," Wertheimer adds. To further clarify the issue, he noted, "They may know restaurants but not student dining. When you are doing student dining, it is much different than retail dining." From his perspective, if you hire the people with experience, they can process the information much quicker and be able to communicate the information back to the owner much faster because they are not learning it for the first time.

Mary Beth McGrew, noted, "I think technical competence is the most important selection criteria, because without that all of the big ideas and good designs and all the other things can't even begin to work. They have to be competent. Sometimes it is the way people can explain their approach to putting something together. Sometimes it is how they've reviewed a similar project, or how they show an understanding of our project and the issues that might pop up. Not the answers, but the issues. When they show that they are thorough, thoughtful, and professional, they get my attention. Everybody says bring the people that are going to do the work, but those people have to be engaged in the conversation. Other people may set the tone for the firm, but a conversation from the people who we will work with directly will tell you if you can work together."

CSU Fullerton's Bond said, "In one word, I'd say 'fit.' That's what it boils down to—for our particular project and our particular client group. Honestly, by the time you get in the room and we're interviewing you, we know you can do the job. There's no question about whether or not you can do the job. Usually one firm out of the four of five invited stands out, but in a negative way, that says perhaps they shouldn't have been invited. But the other firms are usually very close in qualifications. Factors include connection to the project and the client, vibe, eye contact, communicating, and understanding. It's a little like making a marriage."

Deist, Red Cross, added, "Key selection criteria include previous project experience, staff experience, teamwork, and safety. Show us what you have done in similar facilities."

Fleming County Hospital's Midden, said, "The most important criteria when selecting an A/E/C firm depends on the project itself. In our case, it is important to be familiar with local codes. We also like to work with a one-stop shop; a firm with everybody from interior design to foundations to building design. We also like to deal with somebody at the principal level, so if we need something we can go to one person versus a team of people. That is important to us.

According to Midden, "It all comes down to communications. Through the selection process, the most effective approach is sitting down and having a conversation. A big elaborate show is not why we're here. We're here to look at what you can do and what you are going to tell me."

Gateway College's Hughes added, "The process comes down to, 'has the team responded to our description of what it is we think we need'? When you get to the shortlist, every firm and every member of the team can do the work. For me, it is 'have you responded'? The other thing I would say is have you done your homework? I am shocked at how often I've never heard from one of them. Usually they don't survive. Express the desire to know more than what is on the written page. Because, at the end of the day, they can all do the work, but do they want my work?"

Dr. Hughes concluded, "It's not what you did yesterday; it's what you are doing for me tomorrow."

What are the most effective and least effective approaches to offer design and construction services to you?

Most interviewed appreciate the interest expressed by the non-technical marketing professional, who brings social skills and enthusiasm to the first meetings, rather than a more technical individual who tends to try and solve problems before they are fully understood or vetted for priority. Some institutions' representatives, however, see the peer-to-peer relationship with another professional as the foundation for building understanding and trust. Killian said, "Building a relationship is critical. Follow through. Do what you say. Build trust. Where I have a problem is with those who don't follow through. They come and talk, but expect me to take the next step. After they get a project, I like to see them be more proactive than reactive. The firms that bring new insight proactively are those that I value most."

Library Director Fender was clear on what was ineffective, saying, "The people who come in and expect to get the work without having done their homework are the ones that I find the least effective. They know nothing about us; they know nothing about the project; they know nothing about the process, but they expect me to give them a million dollar contract, and that is just not going to happen."

Fender observed that another ineffective approach is when they do ask for statements of qualifications, they receive very minimal or incomplete packages. She said, "This is your chance to make your big pitch of why you should be the firm selected." She noted that the ineffective firms send something that says 'we have been in business here for 100 years and we've done lots of work and you should hire us.' Fender added, "That approach is not going to survive the scrutiny."

Stan Horrell added, "I like people and it's rare to find someone I can't do business with. But it comes down to suitability to the task. I would rather meet people at a trade show or event than in a scheduled meeting. We are a little different than many institutions in that we have a general request for professional services every five years to pre-qualify a group of A/E/C firms, so that we don't have to go back to our board of governors every time we have a new project. It is difficult on an initial basis because we have already defined our preferred group."

Jay Bond shared, "Sometimes it pays to be clever or creative. A principal from a local design firm was interviewing for a project in a typical dry conference room with PowerPoint for the selection committee, telling us why his firm was the best for the job. However, at the end of the interview, in summing up, he said, 'Just to demonstrate that we will go to any heights to make this a successful job...,' and, in one move, he jumped up on to the conference table and landed on both feet. He stuck his landing, and raised his arms and said, 'This is how much we want this project.' Talk about taking a risk. That could have gone badly if he'd fallen or broken the table. He got the job and served us admirably. He showed a willingness to take a risk."

University of Cincinnati's McGrew, added, "It's probably different for different disciplines. There is that bonding with someone from having a conversation that might open the door to a comfort level with doing some work. Then there is annoying marketing. Because I get 150 emails a day, blanket emails don't work. Periodic emails of 'this is who we are and this is what we are doing' still work for me. I do keep those when they relate to a problem I know we might have on campus."

McGrew noted, "For architecture, the booklets are more effective than emails. For engineering, I'm not always looking for a beautiful brochure, but more when someone has done an interesting teaming arrangement that has solved a particular problem. I believe that architecture is about ideas. From the engineer, I want to see how the system fits. It's funny; I have less of a bias for emails from engineers than I do from architects."

Howard Wertheimer commented on what he has seen at Georgia Tech since the recession in 2008. "Because the marketplace has changed...those that haven't been in higher education, are knocking on my door... Maybe they had better partner with a firm who has done student housing, and maybe that firm is not local—a national expert—so the sum of the parts is greater than the whole."

Wertheimer acknowledged the successes he has seen on his campus with strategic teaming of design teams, but he warned, "It needs to be a targeted approach and focused approach to celebrate their expertise." For Wertheimer, however, it all comes back to relationships. "You have to plant those seeds and you have to water them. It may be a slow-growing and long-duration process," Wertheimer said. He knows from personal experience as an architect how a strong relationship can turn a second place finish into the final designer. "We actually got hired because we came in second and maintained those relationships. In some cases the winning firm stumbled, and we'd get a call saying 'would you guys be interested?' You want to maintain the relationships even if you don't win the project. You don't want to chase projects; you want to chase relationships," Wertheimer emphasized.

Kim Fender agreed, saying, "To be effective, the service firm needs to make a really compelling case of why we should hire them. If they provide good case studies and good references, if their submission is well prepared, professional in appearance, and really shows they understood the challenges that we are facing, we are more interested. At the end of the day, anyone can give you a glossy pretty picture and tell us all the great things they are going to do and that they're responsive. When they do all those things, it has really paid off for us."

Jay Bond noted, "Marketing calls can be annoying, but a simple call to acknowledge something they've seen about our university, or to check on the progress of a project that has been announced, is an effective way to keep in front of me. That demonstrates appropriate level of interest."

Bond added, "Any number of times, someone will come in and whine about not getting work, or 'we've been in town for twenty years and you've never called us.' It puts me on the defensive. It does nothing to further their cause. I have much less tolerance for a whiny attitude. We are the owner and have the luxury to be that way. It needs to be about us. First impression is important. If they whine, they rarely come back."

Alternative Delivery Models

Each of the clients represented commented on the rapidly evolving choices for project delivery and their impact on team selection. Continued shrinking funding resources, declining cost of technology, and increased access to data is allowing selection decision making to be more quantitative than qualitative to maximize value for each increasingly limited dollar.

The "Great Recession" has profoundly set new "normal" limits to the public sector owners' abilities to afford services.

"University Architect McGrew, said, "When you talk about rising costs in higher education—that is a runaway train. I think there will be increased financial pressure to use more developer-driven projects. I know that's a reality. It might be faster, it might be quicker, it might meet your budget today, but I haven't seen one yet with long-term staying power. I think as we get more sophisticated, people may begin to understand that in the business of higher education the payback is not five years, it's fifty. Ultimately, I feel we owe our campus buildings not just today, tomorrow, or five years from now—that is all exciting—but fifty years from now."

Rapidly evolving and more frequently preferred project delivery methods like design-build, construction manager-at risk (CMAR), and integrated project delivery (IPD) tripartite contracts are being reviewed and evaluated for their ability to deliver projects cheaper, better, and faster. The tradition of multi-disciplinary design-bid-build (then litigate) contractual models seem to be on the wane. As a result, the A/E/C business developer will need to be knowledgeable and articulate about the value and benefit that their organization can deliver through those alternative contracting models.

Fleming Hospital's Midden, said "In my opinion, the least effective project delivery method is design-build. In the hospital industry, we are fluid. With a design-build project, you may get speed, but a lot of the little details seem to be left in the wake. Quality is very important and sometimes with low-bid, sometimes you get what you pay for. Sometimes you have to live with the budget, whatever it is."

Jay Bond, said, "Rather than the traditional 'hire the designer,' then a year and half later, seek the builder, more and more we are using alternative delivery. We have had a few projects where, because of institutional mandates, we had to use design-bid-build, but those did not go as well as our design-build or CMAR projects. Although in some ways the architect is giving up some control, these alternate delivery approaches seem to deliver a better, on time, and on budget project. If you are looking out ten years, IPD[10] looks very promising. While we haven't done a project under an IPD

---

[10] Integrated Project Delivery is a collaborative alliance of people, systems, business structures, and practices into a process that harnesses the talents and insights of all participants to optimize project results, increase value to the owner, reduce waste, and maximize efficiency through all phases of design, fabrication, and construction.

contract yet, if you look at some of the published projects, it looks positive. I think it looks like it has a lot of promise."

Stan Horrell added, "We are definitely looking at alternative delivery methods like design-build, CMAR, and IPD. But the biggest trend I see for community colleges, and likely for state universities, will be to try to do work with firms only from within our region. It makes no sense for an institution like ours that serves a four county area to look outside that region for professional services."

George Killian noted, "My preferred delivery model is CMAR. I don't see that changing in time. It's a bit of a forced marriage, but it gives us better control of both the architect and the construction manager. We don't have a great track record with design-build, but that has more to do with our inexperience in that model. I'm intrigued by IPD. I think it reinforces that 'blended approach' model I described earlier. The best teams of the future will combine disciplines. Owners are getting smarter. We want to know that the professional service firms are making recommendations that are based on solid research and best practices, not just to try something cutting edge."

Gateway Community College's Hughes, added, "I see design-build as a future delivery model. Design-bid-build is a horrible waste of time and resources. I don't think the selection process would change if design-build were accepted. You would just add the contractor to your team."

He further noted, "For us in public education, building in the future is going to be a lot different. We are looking at putting together funding sources that we've never used before. We use state dollars, we use direct dollars that we can create ourselves, and we use philanthropy. Now we are starting to see private, public-private partnerships, and tax credits. That involves private entities and creating purpose driven corporations. I just think that is going to be the future."

Wertheimer recognizes the continued influence of technology on the design and construction process, and the ability to team successfully. "Technology has fostered that capability because whether you are sitting in the next cubicle or the next stats...distance is a non-issue...Most of the time it works extraordinarily well." Wertheimer sees this continuing to evolve in the industry. "If you are doing a project in Atlanta, Georgia, there is nothing to say that the cost estimating can't be done here and halfway around the world...getting twenty hours of production in a twenty-four hour day."

Kim Fender pointed out the ultimate truism about the future, saying, "I don't know that there are any trends that will influence it. Funding will always drive how much we are able to do."

Midden added, "Price is always going to drive where the health care industry is going. So maximizing effective use of the budget is important. Our business processes change almost every day. We're always looking to increase our market share and what services we can provide—what can we do to help our patients and the people around us. We'll always be looking for the biggest bang for our buck and the best quality for the buck."

As you look forward to the next ten years, what trends and considerations will most influence how you purchase design and construction services?

At the end of the day, the old adage "it's a relationship business" remains the fundamental truth about business development with clients in the public sector. Those relationships are based on shared interests for the success of the client's institution, project delivery, and high levels of communication—all of which ultimately lead to trust, value perception, and long-term opportunities to continue to serve.

There was a consensus that there will always be a role for the A/E/C business developer as a researcher, relationship builder, and conduit for information between the client organization and the provider's firm. That role, however, will require increasing amounts of technical knowledge—not only social skills—if business developers are to be taken seriously and play an important role in the project engagement and delivery process.

The continuing growth of social media venues as a communication vehicle for gathering information, recommendations, and research was cited as important. A web presence is no longer enough. Firms will need to promote expertise in a wider variety of media, and be seen as true thought leaders, not just another firm providing like services.

CSU's Jay Bond noted, "I do think there will be a continuing role for the non-technical marketer or business developer, but the industry is changing. Technical knowledge is becoming more important."

Taylor, Red Cross, added, "The value of a business developer is to bring clarity and understanding of our requirements—brainstorming client needs before they come to the table. There is no replacement for a good technical background and an understanding of the resources we need for this project."

Howard Wertheimer acknowledged the unique skills of a good business developer saying, "Rainmaking is really important. It is a skill that not everybody has...You can only go so far as a technical person...but if you can make rain and bring in work, then your career is unlimited." Wertheimer points out, however, that a strict business developer is limited in that, "Business development people coach their team, but they are superfluous in winning the work. At the end of the day, it is the senior executive, design professional, project manager, or principal...that are going to win the work when you get to the interview."

University of Cincinnati's McGrew added, "I appreciate the people who can quickly address a few of the trends and a similar experience. That is helpful because all you want to know is that we are thinking of the future. Not that the future is always better, but you know where we are headed. It's an interesting time."

Jay Bond concluded, saying it best, "We are all in this together and will share in the success or failure. Stronger owners are taking stronger roles, and the professional service firm needs to be up to the task of participating as part of a multi-disciplinary collaborative team."

Conclusions and Summary

Across the institutional landscape of public sector education, health care, and other not-for-profit organizations, costs for delivery of services are rising, demand for services is growing, funding resources are declining, and competition from the for-profit sector is increasing. Over the next decade, these issues will be compounded by global factors including a population with an increasing lifespan that is redefining the nature of education, the demand for health services, and the increasing importance of philanthropic resources. Simultaneously, the growth of social networking is driving demand for new forms of relationship development and service delivery. Increasing global interconnectivity is putting diversity and adaptability at the center of organizational operations.[11]

Further impacting the ability of the A/E/C professional to position, pursue, and secure new work in the public sector is the unprecedented impact of the global economic downturn that began in 2008, which in many geographic and service sectors, continues to this day. This worldwide monetary contraction has forced a decline in government funding support for public institutions.

Not surprisingly, the representatives from the institutions we approached share similar values and perspectives on what A/E/C services are required, and what influences can help a service provider stand out. Public and non-profit organizations tend—like federal, state, and local

---

[11] Institute for the Future, *Future Work Skills 2020*. Retrieved from http://apolloresearchinstitute.com/research-studies.

government agencies—to put a high value on a qualifications-based selection process.

Even in those instances where a group of qualified firms is identified for a multi-year delivery task order contract, the select pool is initially determined through an RFQ response. In some instances, for projects of low dollar value, a direct-select procedure may be used for contracting A/E/C services. They tend to follow the pre-qualification process and are not bid (low-cost) based.

Changes in the client's service delivery models—from higher education's move toward massive, open online courses and their impact on expanding access and enrollment; to health care's focus on adapting to new federally-mandated financial models and evidence-based design; to non-profit agencies, like the Red Cross' focus on more hardened facilities in response to recent years' disasters in order to ensure they can deliver on promised service levels—are all creating new opportunities for the A/E/C community to, in turn, be of professional service in new ways.

Public institutions—where stakeholders are varied and diverse and fiscal responsibility is critical to long-term success—provide a stable client type that provides a consistent flow of projects for A/E/C firms to serve. They may vary in approach to team selection based on project size and complexity, but they are not so bureaucratic as to be immune from developing strong relationships with service providers.

To be successful in the public sector, business developers must develop a broad technical understanding, take the time to understand the client's organization and needs first, and demonstrate how their firm delivers quality service, communicates information that is of true value, and acts in the best interest of the client.

11 SUPPORTERS
Not-for-Profits

Researcher/Author: Kathryn Hews, CPSM

Analysts/Editors: Kim Icenhower, FSMPS, CPSM; Adam Kilbourne, CPSM

Definition

Special owner not-for-profit organizations are some of the most recognized groups throughout the world. The good deeds and humanitarian contributions made by these organizations are well documented. And yet, for many firms within the design and construction industry, not-for-profit organizations are not considered as part of the client pool during the strategic planning process. Surprisingly, though, when you take a closer look, many of these organizations have robust design and construction budgets, and require virtually all of the services provided through the design and construction industry.

Research Design

The primary research included telephone interviews with nine representatives of not-for-profit organizations, and three interviews with design and construction firms. The primary research was supported by secondary research, conducted through Internet searches of not-for-profit websites, IRS filings, scholastic studies, not-for-profit management sites, etc. Please refer to the source list at the end of this chapter for more information on source materials.

The National Center for Charitable Statistics divides not-for-profits into three basic categories, as summarized the following table.

Not-for-Profit Organizations Overview[1]

501(c)(3) Public Charities		501(c)(3) Private Foundations	Other Exempt Organizations
Arts, higher education, hospitals, human services and more		• **All** must register and file	501(c)(4) Social Welfare
Registered with IRS	Gross receipts $25,000 or more – **Filing IRS Form 990.** Examples: hospitals, college, human services, museums and more	• Most rely on investment income	• 100 or so big HMOs or managed health plants
	Small (under $25,000). Examples: community theaters, neighborhood organizations, new organizations and more	• Only 3,000 of 100,000 have staff, but these account for vast majority of assets	• Mix of advocacy groups, civil clubs
	Congregations (registration voluntary)	• A small percent are "operating foundations," but most are "grantmaking foundations"	501(c)(5) Labor unions, farm bureaus and more
Un-registered	Two primary categories: • Very small organizations (gross receipts under $5,000) • Congregations	• Most are "family foundations"	501(c)(6) Business leagues 501(c)(7) Social and recreational clubs 15-20 other small categories include veterans organizations, fraternal organizations, cemetery companies, and credit unions

Not-for-profit organizations can make a profit, or engage in profit-making activities; however, they are prohibited from passing along any profits to those individuals who control the organization, i.e., boards of trustees, directors, employees, etc. Not-for-profits are able to pay reasonable salaries to officers, employees, and others who perform service for the organization. All of the not-for-profits researched in this chapter fall into the IRS category of 501(c)(3).

According to the IRS, "An organization may qualify for exemption from federal income tax if it is organized and operated exclusively for specific purposes ranging from religious to scientific to the arts. These organizations are involved in the following major categories:

- Religious
- Charitable
- Scientific
- Testing for public safety
- Literary
- Educational

[1] National Center for Charitable Statistics, http://nccsdataweb.urban.org/pubApps/nonprofit-overview.php.

- Fostering national or international amateur sports competition (but only if none of its activities involve providing athletic facilities or equipment)
- The prevention of cruelty to children or animals

The top 25 not-for-profit organizations total revenue ranges from $5.9 billion to almost $700 million. The following chart lists the top 25 not-for-profit organizations in 2011.[2]

| Name | 2011 Total Revenue (,000) | Sources of Income | | | | | In Kind Cont. (,000) |
		Public Support (,000)	Gov't (,000)	Invest. (,000)	Program Service (,000)	Other (,000)	
1. YMCA of the USA	5,986,057	823,404	625,075	43,544	4,428,599	65,435	n/a
2. Goodwill Industries International	4,436,965	777,987	492,098	66,342,890	3,100,537	0	0
3. Catholic Charities USA	4,422,815	679,329	2,993,264	76,8645	488,761	184,596	0
4. United Way	4,139,537	3,903,601	242,043	(6,108)	0	0	218,558
5. American Red Cross	3,452,960	945,868	68,005	52,283	2,328,895	57,919	12,405
6. The Salvation Army	3,203,811	1,697,629	351,489	399,799	146,657	608,237	0
7. Habitat for Humanity International	1,490,611	619,327	247,462	48,464	351,550	223,808	0
8. Boys & Girls Clubs of America	1,458,282	658,324	501,130	5,422	199,481	93,925	56,878
9. Easter Seals	1,402,532	161,598	278,044	11,608	673,131	278,150	5,575
10. Smithsonian Institute	1,240,978	161,385	878,796	51,437	90,321	59,039	6,653
11. Feeding America	1,185,003	1,144,536	0	1,320	19,820	19,327	639
12. Task Force for Global Health	1,163,444	1,147,767	15,660	17	0	0	0
13. Planned Parenthood Federation of America	1,154,000	279,600	470,400	17,400	373,500	13,100	2,700
14. World Vision	1,055,753	848,214	198,654	3,489	4,830	567	505
15. Dana-Farber Cancer Institute	1,002,464	275,765	164,906	332	540,815	20,647	0
16. The Nature Conservancy	997,038	504,032	149,420	100,605	232,038	10,944	22,810
17. Shriners Hospitals for Children	963,647	195,681	1,594	669,350	66,935	30,087	0
18. American Cancer Society	953,576	888,314	25,916	18,640	0	20,706	50,578
19. Food for the Poor	938,211	930,202	8,016	22	0	(29)	0
20. Boy Scouts of America	904,686	393,994	4,485	7,997	324,250	173,960	n/a
21. Catholic Relief Services	821,539	319,364	497,171	8,635	57	(3,688)	276
22. ALSAC/St. Jude's Children's Research Hospital	814,333	698,411	0	90,069	0	25,853	0
23. Children's Hospital Los Angeles	812,806	97,695	44,254	18,436	649,765	2,656	0
24. Girl Scouts of the USA	735,232	102,277	6,498	18,621	518,615	89,221	6,831
25. YMCA	699,911	397,651	287,245	n/a	n/a	302,260	n/a

To qualify, the organization must be a corporation, community chest fund, articles of association, or foundation.[3]

Maintaining the Spirit of Giving

Despite the global economic slowdown of 2006-2010, the total not-for-profit sector has actually shown steady growth since 1999. The number of reporting non-profits grew 48 percent between 1999 and 2009, with $1.87

[2] The Non-Profit Times. November 1, 2012. Page 4.
[3] Department of the Treasury, Internal Revenue Service. "Tax-Exempt Status for Your Organization." Publication 557 (Rev. October 2011). Page 23.

trillion in revenue and $4.3 trillion in assets in 2009. After adjusting for inflation, revenues of reporting non-profits grew 34 percent, expenses grew 51 percent, and assets grew 39 percent in the same period. The number of registered public charities grew 59 percent during this same period, while the number of reporting public charities grew 47 percent. In 2010, total private giving reached approximately $291 billion, up 2 percent from the revised estimate for 2009, after adjusting for inflation.[4]

According to The NonProfit Times (NPT), public support for the nation's largest charities increased only slightly in 2011. However, the percentage of revenue shrank as the NPT Top 100 organizations focused on generating program service revenue. Investment income overall was generally flat, and more charities were affected by continued declines in federal and state government support. Organizations in the annual NPT Top 100 report had public support of $33.4 billion, falling below 50 percent of their total revenue of $66.9 billion. The same 100 organizations saw public support of $33.2 billion amid overall revenue of $65.4 billion in 2010, almost 51 percent. With declining support from government and weaker charitable giving from a smaller pool of donors, the nation's largest non-profits have turned to other revenue streams, e.g., increased requests of United Way, higher membership dues, increased giving of food or materials from large retailers.[5]

Is working with a special owner, not-for-profit good for our firm?

Working with a not-for-profit organization can be rewarding to both parties, if the expectations for the relationship are clearly understood from the outcome. Al Potter of Gilbane said, "There are a bunch of criteria we take into account when we decide to pursue a not-for-profit project. First and foremost, is there funding? Everyone likes to work for non-profits as they typically have a nice humanitarian sense in their mission. Whether it is a charitable organization doing good works, or a humanitarian organization, or if it is structured for a particular mission, it's easy to become engaged with the mission. But, with that, we need to make sure that the project is funded and that we don't get too far down the road providing a bunch of services that are not funded."

If a design and construction firm is interested in adding a not-for-profit organization to their client portfolio, there is considerable and timely information available from secondary sources. Representative secondary sources including IRS tax filings, annual reports, not-for-profit websites, and numerous organizations, both public and private, designed to assist not-for-profits in achieving their mission.

---

[4] National Center for Charitable Statistics at the Urban Institute. "The Non-Profit Sector in Brief." 2011.
[5] The NonProfit Times, "NPT 2012 Top 100," 1 November 2012.

The not-for-profit sector is highly regulated and scrutinized, not only by the government, but also by their respective boards of trustees, and by their donors whom they rely on heavily for funding.

There are websites that track how much of a donor's dollar actually goes to achieving the organizations' mission. There are other websites that report on how much the leadership of an organization is compensated. The first step before entering into a relationship with a not-for-profit organization is taking the time to conduct secondary research into the organization.

During a design and construction firm's strategic planning process, if working with a not-for-profit organization is under consideration, the marketing department can provide background information to make an informed decision. Among the key questions to find answers for are:

- What is the organization's background and mission statement?
- How is the organization structured? Are they a local branch of a larger organization?
- What are their revenue streams (e.g., public funding, private donors, foundation grants, other)?
- Who is their leadership and who are their key decision makers?
- Has the not-for-profit leadership worked with designers or constructors in the past, and if so, how did that relationship work out?
- What services could our firm provide to the not-for-profit, and what advantages do we bring?
- Do we have an internal champion to pursue this organization, and will senior management support this initiative?
- Does our core value system align with the not-for-profit's mission?

"Most non-profits, even larger ones, often hesitate to spend money on administrative overhead, such as consultants or other outside experts, because this is seen as diverting valuable dollars from direct service. Of course, most non-profits have no choice. They don't have enough money to even consider hiring consultants at for-profit rates. Low-cost, volunteer-based assistance often is an appropriate solution."[6]

---

[6] Free Management Library. Basic Overview of Nonprofit Organizations.

Understanding the Mission

As noted earlier, not-for-profit organizations have a wide variety of missions. The not-for-profit sector organizations have become essential to the fabric of our communities.

Interviews were conducted with nine not-for-profit senior leaders, representing six different organizations. Several individuals with Catholic Charities and the YMCA, both in the top 5 of the Top 25 Not-for-Profit Organizations, were interviewed to gain both a regional perspective and a greater understanding of the types of programs and building programs in which they had participated. An objective was to get a good geographic representation, as well as a wide range of the missions covered by these different organizations.

The organizations represented in this chapter can trace their histories as far back as 1727, when the Ursuline sisters arrived from France to open an orphanage, school for street girls, and health facility in New Orleans as the first formal Catholic Charity in the United States.

The newest organization, the Humane Society of the United States (HSUS), dates back to 1954, but the organization's roots actually trace back to 1866 with the establishment of the Society for the Prevention of Cruelty to Animals (SPCA). The HSUS broke off from the successor organization to the SPCA in 1954 to focus on protection of animals through advocacy, education, and hands-on programs.

United Way can trace its roots back to 1887 when a Denver woman, a priest, two ministers and a rabbi recognized the need for cooperative action to address their city's welfare problems and created an organization to serve as an agent to collect funds for local charities, as well as to coordinate relief services, counsel and refer clients to cooperating agencies, and make emergency assistance grants in cases which could not be referred. That year, Denver raised $21,700 and created a movement that would spread throughout the country to become the United Way.

The Save the Redwoods League was created through the foresight of Stephen Mather, head of the National Parks Service, who in 1917 convinced conservationists John C. Merriam, Madison Grant, and Henry Fairfield Osborn, to investigate the state of the redwood forests in Northern California. Grant worked with Merriam and others to form Save the Redwoods League in 1918, pledging $100 toward the effort.

In the creation of all of these organizations, a need was recognized, a statement of mission written, and an organization to fulfill the mission formed. And finally, the Morton Arboretum was founded in 1922. At that time, three focus areas were put into place—the living plant collections, a research library, and an herbarium. The education program was added in 1940, a formal research program was established, and the Sterling Morton Library was built in 1963.

Understanding an organization's mission is a key to establishing a successful working relationship with a not-for-profit.

The representatives interviewed from not-for-profit organizations include the following:

- Catholic Charities USA (CCUSA): Candy Hill, Senior VP for Social Policy and Government Affairs
- Catholic Charities Housing and Catholic Charities of the Diocese of Yakima: John Young, President and CEO
- Catholic Charities of the Archdiocese and Catholic Housing Development Corporation of Chicago: Monsignor Michael Boland, President and CEO
- YMCA of Greater Boston: Joseph Barry, Director of Property Management
- YMCA of Metropolitan Dallas: Gordon Echtenkamp, President
- United Way of Greater Portland (Maine): Suzanne McCormick, Executive Director
- Humane Society of the United States: Melissa Rubin, Vice President of Animal Care Centers
- Save the Redwoods League: Catherine Elliott, Land Project Manager
- Morton Arboretum: Kris Bachtell, Director of Collections

The individual interviews lasted between twenty-five and fifty minutes, and followed a questionnaire format. All respondents expressed interest in learning how their peers worked with design and construction firms.

What We Learned About Not-for-Profits Mission and Structure

According to the respondents, the most important elements to achieving their missions ranged from membership satisfaction, to doing what is best for the recipients of their services, to building the needed housing or facilities that meet the organizations' missions. Successful fundraising

For Catholic Charities, the mission of the organization has shifted from being output driven—e.g., number of nights in shelter, or number of meals served—to getting people out of poverty and sustaining themselves.

Candy Hill said, "CCUSA has created legislative language, and the president of CCUSA wrote a book on the economic breakdown in the United States, and how the situation provides an opportunity to take a new look at dealing with entrenched poverty. These are lofty goals. But, we feel we have the credibility and experience to be part of the national discourse to change the system. We have taken a lot of steps to achieve our mission."

All of the organizations have an executive director or president, and are overseen by a board of directors or advisors, ranging in size from a ten-member board, to a more than sixty-member board of directors. In addition, several of the organizations have outside advisors or experts to assist in the technical aspects of their organizations.

Capital planning for the organizations tends to be updated annually, and any expenditure is heavily dependent on the success of fundraising. According to Gordon Echtenkamp, President of the YMCA of Metropolitan Dallas, "We send out a wish list for each branch in October, and each branch puts items on the list for the following year, and assigns a "need" number. That list is then taken into the finance and facility group who oversees the capital plan, and they weed through and decide what can be done. We have a certain dollar amount for each year that is dedicated to capital projects, and we work to get the dollars to match."

The HSUS has a longer-range plan. As Melissa Rubin shared, "We recently developed a ten year plan. All five of our animal care centers are being looked at, particularly the Black Beauty ranch. We created a 'Vision Plan' of what we would need to build as far as infrastructure. This facility hasn't had visitors before, so we needed to figure out what infrastructure would be needed. Our Vision Plan identified what we would have in an ideal world, and who to reach out to for developing the infrastructure."

The organizations felt the effects of the economic downturn, but surprisingly less than other segments of the economy. According to Catherine Elliott, of Save the Redwoods League, "I don't know that it has. We've been aware of it, and I don't have statistics on it, and some donors might not have had as much to give. But, we have very committed donors. We keep our staff level at thirty. We are very conservatively run, and a smart organization."

For other organizations, the major result of the economic downturn has been a drop in public funding or a decrease in donations. However, each of the organizations has been proactive in expanding membership or seeking other sources of funding to offset any impacts.

How Have Design and Construction Firms Performed?

All of the respondents interviewed had experience working with design and construction firms, ranging from new construction to renovations to design-build projects for development of YMCA facilities. Past experience working with the organization is frequently an important consideration, or at least experience working in a similar field or similar facility, and local presence can be important criteria.

According to Joe Barry of the YMCA of Greater Boston, "I think the knowledge of a YMCA gymnasium is the most important criteria. We have a certain clientele and the design team has to have experience in a fitness atmosphere, with locker rooms, gymnasiums, the types of features that our clientele are looking for. The pool is a big deal. We work with only one pool manufacturer, and we expect our architects to work with them."

Experience with regulators or permitting agencies is very important to not-for-profits. Also, not-for-profits are very conscious of past performance, and they check references carefully.

"The most important criteria we consider are quality, references, integrity, and cost. Reputation is very important. And whoever we select has to believe in our mission. It has to be someone who has the vision to understand what we are trying to build, but they also have to be someone who really believes in what we are doing. I've run into problems with people who don't understand what we are all about," said HSUS's Melissa Rubin.

Kris Bachtell, Morton Arboretum, said, "Our selection process is like what most people would do, even for home remodeling. We look at the team's expertise. Are they focused on what you need, whether it is a building or a parking lot. We look at reputation, ask for references, and we look at the jobs they've done. Is it the same context as what we are building? And then, price is a decision point, but that is three, four, or five down the line. We are more interested in their level of expertise, and in areas working specifically where you need them. Do you like their architecture, things like that, and then cost comes into play. And then we look at how they are in interviews. Are they arrogant, or are they thoughtful? You get a sense of their culture from the interview."

"When we select a designer, I think it is important to have someone who would work with us to understand how work flows in our organization, and who takes the time to learn what is important to staff within the space. We would want someone who spends time getting input into what we really care about in our workplace," said Suzanne McCormick, United Way of Greater Portland.

Most design and construction firms who have worked with not-for-profits in the past have met the organization's expectations. Listening, being proactive, providing thoughtful designs, and understanding the mission, were all highlighted as reasons for meeting expectations.

Monsignor Michael Boland, Catholic Charities of Chicago said, "Our expectations are that the design or construction entity will deliver the building on time, and to do everything else that we would expect as outlined in our RFP. This has been something of a challenge in dealing with architects. We need to make sure that they can provide high quality services to the poor. We've found that the architects sometimes think the final product can be built cheaper, when it really can't. Our expectations of the final product are the same as in the private sector."

Areas where design and construction firms can improve services are in minimizing change orders during construction, being more realistic about the organization's budget and expectations, and offering a wider range of options and materials. Also of value is providing more practical designs to anticipate future maintenance and repair needs.

Joseph Barry, YMCA of Greater Boston said, "In the design, we could look at a better range of projects. I'm sure things were value engineered and probably downgraded to meet our budget, but I'd like to look at a wider range of projects, and to include longevity in the mix. We are around for a long time and don't want things that only last two or three years."

There were several suggestions for additional services that would be of value to not-for-profit organizations.

For some, educating the organization about different types of delivery methods, e.g., design-build or turnkey services, would be of value.

Developing a standard contract—particularly one that addressed change orders—would also benefit the not-for-profit. For other organizations, keeping abreast of regulatory or scientific trends is important.

"Our funders are asking about climate change. We had a major donor who went to a conference on local climate change, and how climate change will affect things on a local level rather than a global level. I don't know a contractor who knows more than I do yet about climate change, but we all need to be thinking about that," said Catherine Elliott, Save the Redwoods League.

How to create more efficient workplaces for organizations that have high numbers of field personnel was also mentioned as a future need.

Suzanne McCormick, United Way of Greater Portland, said, "One of the changes that have occurred since I've moved into my position is that I have been trying to make more staff work out of the office and in the field, to be more mobile. Within the next ten years we might need less space. How do we downsize space, but still have functionality? We might want to maximize the current state of virtual work in our workplace. That's been something that I've been observing. We frequently have a lot of empty desks when staff are in the field. So I'm asking myself, is this still the right configuration of space for us."

Interacting with Not-for-Profits

The individuals interviewed want to interact with a principal, project manager, creative person, or architect/engineer of record. There were mixed responses when asked if there was a role for non-technical marketers and business developers seeking to provide services to the organization. On the one hand, there was recognition that involvement of marketers and business developers was expected. On the other hand, there is concern that a non-technical marketer or business developer would not necessarily understand the organization.

Gordon Echtenkamp, YMCA of Metropolitan Dallas, said, "I suspect the marketers and business developers have to be involved. Rainmakers need to bring the big guys into the room. With the limited number of principals in a firm, they have to have others telling the story of what the company offers. There is a parallel in the Y. I'm the one who has to go into the room to solicit funds, but I'm limited in how much ground I can cover. There has to be other door openers."

Catherine Elliott said, "I tend to think there is not a role for non-technical marketers and business developers. That's not because they aren't fine, but we tend to connect on the technical side, so what the consulting team can provide is usually understood at that level. We want to work with someone who has a good reputation on that type of project; we want to talk to a good implementer of an environmental service."

Effective approaches to interacting with not-for-profits ranged from formal presentations, to networking at professional association events, to setting up a meeting with the development staff. Cold calling is not a welcome approach. Doing homework about the organization and understanding the mission is expected.

"The more you know about us culturally, the better off you will be. It's more than just reading. For us, the buildings are only tools. The resources are best spent on the kids, not on building big structures. That's the necessary evil that we have to endure in order to achieve our mission. Some people in the design industry look at their output as art. I'm in the business of impacting lives. That's the biggest learning curve for someone wanting to work in our industry is understanding why we do this. If I had my druthers, I wouldn't have buildings, I would use others' facilities. What we do is not nearly as important as why we do it," said Gordon Echtenkamp, YMCA of Metropolitan Dallas.

This sentiment was echoed by John Young of Catholic Charities Housing of Yakima: "We not only develop our housing, but we also own and manage our developments. We have the ongoing relationship with the local community, the mayor, the schools. We can talk about the impact on the quality of life. But we also clearly can speak about the economic impact of our housing development. We can quantify how many jobs we have created through our developments. We can quantitatively talk about that. Long gone is the desire to just do nice things. We also need to talk about our responsibility as stewards."

In addition to the nine interviews with representatives from not-for-profit organizations, three individuals from design and construction firms were interviewed to gain perspective on how they decide to pursue opportunities with not-for-profit organizations.

The three individuals are: Gilbane Building Company: Alfred K. Potter, FSMPS, Senior Vice President and Director of Business Development, Federal Sector; ESA/PWA: Lisa Crossett, Corporate Marketing and Communications Director; and Sasaki Associates: Michael Potter, Senior Associate.

All of these individuals have had direct experience working with not-for-profits, and in the case of Al Potter and Michael Potter, have served as board members for charitable organizations. For their respective firms, the percentage of revenue generated from not-for-profit organizations is less than 5 percent. The three firms have been involved in very different types of projects. For ESA/PWA, the focus has been on environmental planning, whereas for Gilbane, the focus has been on buildings or monuments. Sasaki Associates has performed a range of services for not-for-profits, including master planning, landscape architecture, permitting, regulatory approvals, etc.

All three individuals highlighted the importance of understanding and embracing the mission of the organization or the project, but also commented they made sure a project was funded before any major work was performed. Pro bono work has been performed for strategic positioning, if the not-for-profit is part of the local community and needs the help, or if there is a relationship building opportunity.

Al Potter, Gilbane Building Company, said, "It could be that they are local in the community and we want to help them because it is the right thing to do. We may have an engagement with the organization, or an employee who does, and we want to assist them. In some cases, there may be a relationship between the non-profit and another client or set of clients that would be profitable for us. Some non-profits have very well-to-do boards that have decision-makers in other employment situations. This might be a low-key way to gain access to a number of other board members or stakeholders."

"I think it's really what connection or resonance we have with the organization. We want to make sure that the organization's mission closely matches what we do. Or, it could be that we know the people involved very closely through existing business relationships and we've been asked or sought out, or we want to support the organization for the sake of our staff. For example, we work with the Town of Watertown as we see this as a great way to benefit the community where a lot of our people work and live," said Michael Potter, Sasaki Associates

One interesting expectation of working with not-for-profits is the type of projects that the organizations are engaged in. Lisa Crossett, ESA/PWA noted, "I think that the difference is that they probably have more interesting projects. That's what you would see with a non-profit. I think you would find that with other kinds of consultants who work with not-for-profits, say education or other markets. A non-profit educational organization will probably be doing more cutting edge stuff, and the people are working with them because the projects are more exciting or interesting."

Sasaki Associates has taken a unique approach to performing pro bono work, and although not necessarily for the not-for-profit sector, could be tailored to a not-for-profit client. Every summer, through its student intern program, Sasaki Associates brings their interns together to design a project, oftentimes for local municipalities.

An example project was work conducted for the City of Chelsea, Massachusetts, to develop concepts for connecting the city around the Tobin Bridge (construction of the bridge in the 1950s divided the city in half). "In encouraging renewal, one of the primary challenges the city faces is the Tobin Bridge, a major highway corridor that bisects the city. The Sasaki team sought opportunities to transform it into a hub of cultural and public activities that celebrate the history of Chelsea. Strategies included eliminating the psychological and physical barrier of the Tobin Bridge, addressing key safety issues of the bridge and surrounding area, and establishing walkable environments. The team hopes these concepts, defined in the Chelsea Vision Plan, will further revitalize Chelsea and reshape the present perception of the city."[7]

As part of its organization, Gilbane has established a Special Projects Group (SPG) as a stand-alone division, to handle projects that may be small in size, but critical in nature. The SPG is brought in to work on selected not-for-profit projects. Al Potter, Gilbane Building Company, said, "For instance, we recently completed a job for the Children's Friend organization, which was under $2 million. This project was executed by our SPG, which has leaner procedures and less administrative oversight."

There are several areas where design and construction firms could enhance services to not-for-profit organizations. As noted earlier, many not-for-profits are engaged in cutting edge research. It is important, therefore, that the design and construction industry remain on top of cutting edge technologies, e.g., climate change, or more extensive use of visualization or BIM. There may be opportunities for stakeholder facilitation, community relations, transition planning, or continuing education for non-profits on the design and construction process so that they are better informed clients.

Al Potter said, "I think that education is important, and by that I mean educating the clients. Being straightforward and honest is important,

---

[7] Sasaki Associates website. Sasaki Design Charrette: Re-envisioning Chelsea. 27 August 2012.

because by definition, the not-for-profit is not as informed as a for-profit who builds buildings on a repeat basis. There is great potential that the client may not be savvy, and therefore the process may not be structured properly. There may be problems during selection, or worse, during the project. Problems are bad for the client and for our firm. We all have integrity and values that we want to manifest, and nowhere more than in dealing with the not-for-profit client, because they need the trustworthy input that we can make to guide them straight. Without that honest input, they can easily be steered wrong. All of this links to educating the not-for-profit client. You need to help them make good decisions, even if you are not selected. They need the tools and knowledge to make a good selection with the right processes and a trusted firm, rather than ending up in an unethical situation."

The most frequent interactions with not-for-profits are at the executive director or at the project manager level. Other key contacts are with the finance director or the facilities manager. In some cases, the not-for-profit has an outside agent, who may be an architect, real estate agent, or a board member with building design or construction experience. "The outside agent can be very helpful to us in explaining to a client how an estimate is done, or how a guaranteed maximum price is assembled, or the importance of safety during a project, or why value engineering should be done, or how to engage DBEs in a professional fashion. These individuals can be very helpful as a trusted resource. They help to validate your role," said Potter.

One particularly effective approach to reaching out to not-for-profits is to participate in academic conferences or seminars. It is important to be seen as the expert, or highly technical advisor. It is also important to be aware of the client's activities so that when a project is in its earliest stages, the design and construction firm can help to shape the scope of work, selection process, and delivery method.

The least effective approach to working with a not-for-profit is to simply respond to an RFP without knowing the background of the organization and their mission, or even worse, to ignore what they are saying when they ask for your services. Lisa Crossett, ESA/PWA, said "I think if we don't listen to them, we'll lose them as clients. When we don't hear what their needs are, we have to maintain their trust by listening to them."

Should We Work with Not-for-Profits?

There are many reasons to work with not-for-profits. Not-for-profit projects can be challenging and cutting edge, and working on these projects can expand a firm's internal capabilities. Presenting what has been learned from these cutting edge projects at professional seminars or conferences can position a firm as an expert in a particular field or service.

Michael Potter, Sasaki Associates, said, "I definitely feel like everything we do now is imbued with more marketing of the firm. As we continue to evaluate working with not-for-profits, we look to create relationships, and how this relationship helps our portfolio. What are the reasons we are pursuing work with this organization? Those are questions we would ask ourselves, rather than just doing the work."

The projects that design and construction industry firms undertake can improve the quality of life of an individual, a group, or a community. Being directly involved with the organization, either as a volunteer or as a board member can enhance a company's reputation within the local community. This is particularly true if a firm is entering a new geographic market and wants to become known.

"It also helps if you care about the mission of the client. Most not-for-profits have a mission and believing in that cause can be very important in demonstrating the passion for the client, and frankly, gets people within our firm excited about the work, which makes it more fun," said Potter.

Conclusions and Summary

Non-for-profit organizations are big business. The top five organizations generate $3.4 billion and above annually and many have existed for literally hundreds of years. Many of these organizations have facilities that require A/E/C services and despite the economic woes of the last several years, the non-for-profit organizations have continued to grow slowly. The larger organizations are structured with an executive director and a board of directors, which can make these projects difficult for A/E/C firms. Firms that have worked for these organizations understand that many times the board needs to be educated on the building process to clearly understand what will be included in the scope. These organizations usually run on razor thin budgets and firms that provide A/E/C services fall into two categories: doing the work pro bono or for a fee, and wanting to give back to the community.

Not-for-profit organizations should be vetted prior to engaging in work. These organizations are highly regulated and there is a lot of information available on the web. Research is to determine if the organization has a reasonable budget, a board of directors, and if the firm's mission and the not-for-profit's mission align. Firms that decided to work with not-for-profit organizations found the work to be challenging and rewarding.

When a not-for-profit organization hires an A/E/C firm, reputation and a passion for their mission is critical, as is expertise. When the A/E/C firm understands the not-for-profit organization's mission and structure, then designs meet the organization needs. A/E/C firms should take the time to educate the organization on the alternative design and construction methods, reduce change orders, and be efficient. Not-for-profit organizations want to be treated like any other private business.

12 BUYERS OF A/E/C SERVICES
Summary of Findings

Researchers/Authors: Scott W. Braley, FAIA, FRSA;
Scott D. Butcher, FSMPS, CPSM

Analysts/Editors: Scott W. Braley, FAIA, FRSA;
Scott D. Butcher, FSMPS, CPSM

Although the research has revealed many distinctive behaviors of A/E/C buyers depending upon their market sector, there are some generalities that became apparent through the process.

In many ways, relationships are still key and buyers like the traditional ways of "selling."

They prefer to work with A/E/C firms with which they already have solid relationships. They strongly dislike being cold called, and many won't meet with any firm trying to give a generic sales presentation. Face-to-face meetings are critical to establishing rapport.

Buyers are not interested in order takers.

Virtually all of the buyers interviewed noted that the day of "show up and take an order" are over. Generally, RFPs are trending toward performance requests. Buyers expect that sellers will offer and suggest more, and ask "what do you want" less. The market is challenging for buyers, as well as sellers, and the buyers point out that "we don't have all the answers anymore."

Business developers must understand the buyer's company or institution and industry.

"Don't even think of contacting me if you don't know about me, my entity and my needs and concerns. I'm not here to educate you—it's the other way around." Similar comments were heard in all sectors. Buyers have limited time available to meet with firms trying to sell them design and construction services, so when they do make the decision to meet with someone, they demand that the business developer calling on them have more than a basic understanding about their organization. While this may not be earthshaking news, the degree to which this is true is a tectonic shift in behavior.

The future for non-technical business developers is questionable.

While the responses varied by segment, buyers in general see a declining role for business developers who don't have technical skills. Moreover, they are quite clear that they want to talk to individuals who will be part of their project team—definitely not business developers who will not be around after selection.

On the positive side, buyers indicated that non-technical business developers frequently have better conversational skills and are better listeners than technical professionals. This means professional and technical staff members must learn the communication skills so common among business developers. The public sector is an exception to this trend. We found that non-technical business developers are more welcome here than in the private sector.

Buyers want you to innovate—and help them innovate in the process.

Across most buyer sectors, interviewees said that they are looking for "leading edge" or "cutting edge" designers and builders. Noting that it is exponentially difficult to differentiate A/E/C firms, buyers said that they look for companies that can demonstrate thought leadership in the industry and specific sector. Buyers reported that some of the first indicators of demonstrated innovation are publishing articles and white papers, or speaking at conferences.

Buyers are experimenting—but not taking big chances—with project delivery.

Buyers are keen to innovate in project delivery through technology integration or evidence-based design. They feel that A/E/C firms that can innovate can actually help the buyers' organizations innovate the products or services they provide to their clients. However, buyers aren't willing to take big risks with project delivery. They are looking for A/E/C firms to educate them on the options, make recommendations, choose innovative delivery approaches with care, and back that up with solid, top-notch project managers who can make success happen.

Some buyers say, "Don't find us, we'll find you."

A recurrent theme in the interviews was that buyers increasingly use the Internet to research A/E/C firms, preferring to find companies that they feel could best help solve their challenges. This growing trend demonstrates the importance of inbound marketing and does reinforce a more global trend: the decline in effectiveness of outbound marketing techniques.

Full-service isn't what it used to be.

While some continue to appreciate the "one-stop-shop" approach, a number of interviewees noted that they use technology to sift through the myriad firms serving any given market segment, and prefer to pick and choose team members (companies or even individuals) that best match their project needs. The trend toward the buyer putting together the project team will continue.

Reputation and references are still the keys to success.

Buyers want to know that a company has been down this path before with similar clients, and they want to talk to those clients about a company's performance. In fact, buyers often contact companies or organizations similar to their own to get referrals for designers and constructors, which again emphasizes the trend: "Don't call us, we'll call you."

Focusing on the buyer's specific project wins the day.

This finding sounds almost too basic to mention; however, just like "don't forget to breathe," buyers still find that A/E/C firms spend too much time talking about themselves, and not enough time talking about the buyer and their project.

Money makes the world go round.

Across all segments, buyers noted that their project workload is generally down, that their funding has been cut, and that any A/E/C firm that can help them find money for their project will be able to differentiate themselves from the competition. This was further evidenced by a growing interest in public-private partnerships.

Local is the new local.

Interestingly, in this day and age of advanced technology and virtual offices, several buyers in different segments noted that they are under increasing pressure to stay with local A/E/C firms. Even when they want or need to cast a wider net for the major projects, they will invariably want to include local participants.

A/E/C firms that offer the most value often go far beyond just design and construction services.

This came out in a number of conversations with buyers, and it relates to several points above—whether helping buyers to innovate their projects or services, finding funding for a project, or educating project stakeholders. In fact, within the state and local government group, a number of buyers specifically stated that they are under the gun to be more transparent, political officials are demanding perfection, and they are looking to their A/E/C firms to help demonstrate to the public why a project is important and what negative things could happen if a project is cancelled. This is one emerging role that buyers felt was ideally suited to the non-technical business developers.

For savvy A/E/C business developers, this research might reinforce some of what they have suspected or experienced. Nonetheless, the Foundation's research is a clarion call to action for A/E/C firms. If you have a poor, out of date website, you are losing work. If your business development program is still geared toward outbound tactics, with little thought to inbound marketing, opportunities for which your firm is qualified are passing you by. If you still go into sales meetings or presentations and spend all the time talking about your company and presenting your portfolio, your chance of success is minimal at best. If you are not demonstrating thought leadership through research and publishing, you are not differentiating your firm. If your company relies on a sales force of non-technical business developers, there is a significant percentage of buyers that won't even meet with your company. If your company is so focused on "doing"—that is, designing or building—your competitors are gaining a competitive advantage over you by helping buyers to innovate their products or services, or helping them to find money to fund their projects.

In some ways, the more things change, the more they stay the same, but make no mistake, things are changing! Buyers want to meet with people in person. They want someone who can solve their problems. They want chemistry and rapport with the design and construction members who will comprise their team. And they simply won't stand for cold calls or generic presentations.

Certain changes that have sprouted in recent years are emerging as dominant forces in the future of business development. For instance, evidence-based design may have originated within the health care sector, but colleges and corporations are now looking for evidence-based decisions, too. Buyers want to be educated. They want business developers to present innovative project delivery options and recommend the most appropriate approach. They want firms to offer value by not "just" designing or constructing. In fact, one of the more salient overarching themes of the SMPS Foundation research is the lessoned role of traditional A/E/C services in delivering a comprehensive project solution.

Legendary General George S. Patton is quoted for saying, "Lead me, follow me, or get out of my way," which is often truncated to the simpler "Lead, follow, or get out of the way." If your A/E/C firm is not leading-edge when it comes to business development methodologies, you should be studying industry innovators and emulating them. Buyers are increasingly sophisticated; they know what the top A/E/C firms are doing, and they now expect this of your firm.

13 BASELINE RESEARCH QUESTIONS

To provide consistency throughout the TLS Committee's primary research work, all research and analysis teams used a uniform set of baseline queries. Regardless of the seller's or buyer's individual focus or disposition, TLS researchers assured that the interviewee addressed the following questions. Similarly, in other data-sourcing and research venues, these questions guided the collection of data and information.

Predictably, and by design, these core baseline questions led to and prompted other questions, comments and discussions that proved invaluable in the primary research data collection and information analysis.

Sellers – Uniform Baseline Questions

- What are your most effective current strategies and approaches to business development as you seek to provide design or construction services?
- How effective are your current strategies and approaches to business development, and how do you see them changing in the next ten years ahead?
- How have you changed your strategies and approaches to business development in recent years, and do you see these changes as short term or permanent in the decade ahead?
- What changes do you plan to make in the next ten years regarding either strategy or approach to business development, and do you see these changes as short term or permanent?

- As you look forward to the next ten years, what trends and considerations will most influence how you conduct business development to offer design and construction services?

Buyers – Uniform Baseline Questions

- What are your expectations of/for design and construction entities seeking to provide design and/or construction to you?
- With whom do you most want to interact when members of the design and construction industry offer you services (e.g., principal, senior executive, project manager, technical staff, marketer, business development representative, etc.)?
- As you envision the decade ahead, is there a role for non-technical marketers and business developers in seeking to provide design and/or construction services to you?
- What are the most important criteria you consider when selecting a provider of design and/or construction services?
- What are the most effective, and least effective, approaches used to offer design or construction services to you?
- As you look forward to the next ten years, what trends and considerations will most influence how you purchase design and construction services?

PART 3 – ABOUT SMPS AND THE SMPS FOUNDATION

14 ABOUT THE SMPS THOUGHT LEADERSHIP COMMITTEE

Compilers/Editors: Vanessa C. Aron; Scott W. Braley, FAIA, FRSA; Scott D. Butcher, FSMPS, CPSM; Amy Villasana-Moore, CPSM

In the fall of 2011 the SMPS Foundation charged Scott Braley and Scott Butcher, both Foundation Trustees, to form and guide an ad hoc research and writing team identified as the "2012-13 Thought Leadership Series (TLS) Committee." As a key element of the Foundation's focus on research, the TLS Committee's work comprised conducting and documenting primary research focused specifically on business development in the design and construction industry.

Based on an open solicitation to SMPS Fellows and CPSMs, the all-volunteer committee came together and began its work in January of 2012. This book represents the culmination of work by almost thirty volunteers on an effort that spanned more than a year.

The SMPS Foundation wishes to acknowledge and thank the many SMPS members and other individuals who comprised the TLS Committee. First and foremost, we thank the research and writing teams whose dedication to this project produced a wealth of valuable material and subsequent critical analysis. We are also much obliged to the editing and manuscript teams for their insight into the final analyses, structuring, and polishing of the publication. Lastly, we thank the TLS leaders as well as the Foundation staff whose guidance and coordination throughout the year kept the committee on track. This entirely volunteer effort is a worthy testament to the commitment and spirit of the SMPS Foundation.

Thank you.

About the Co-Chairs
Scott W. Braley, FAIA, FRSA

Scott W. Braley, FAIA, FRSA, is a design and construction industry strategist, consultant, and trainer. Braley Consulting & Training helps design and construction firms plan strategically, then get work, do work, run the business, and transition leadership/ownership to achieve unprecedented success. Based on more than thirty years in international A/E and CM/PM practice—ten as managing principal in an ENR Top 40 firm—Scott has devoted his full-time energies to consulting since 1998.

Scott served as co-chair for the TLS Committee, as well as Researcher/Author of the Introduction, Directors (Constructors and Construction Managers), and Buyers of A/E/C Services Summary of Findings. Scott also served as Analyst/Editor for Predictables (Public Sector – Federal Government), Compiler/Editor of About the SMPS Foundation Thought Leadership Committee, and provided miscellaneous editing and proofreading throughout the project.

Scott D. Butcher, FSMPS, CPSM

Scott D. Butcher, FSMPS, CPSM, is Vice President and Director of Business Development for JDB Engineering, Inc. and affiliate companies. A Trustee of the SMPS Foundation, he has more than two decades of A/E/C marketing experience, has authored a dozen books, as well as numerous articles about professional services marketing topics. Scott is a CPSM, Fellow of SMPS, and has presented at local, regional, and national A/E/C conferences and events.

Scott served as co-chair for the TLS Committee, as well as Researcher/Author for Collaborators (Sub-consultants and Specialty Consultants), Predictables (Public Sector – Federal Government), and Buyers of A/E/C Services Summary of Findings. Scott also served as Compiler/Editor of About the SMPS Foundation Thought Leadership Committee, and provided miscellaneous editing and proofreading throughout the project.

TLS Committee
Vanessa C. Aron

Vanessa C. Aron is the Marketing Specialist for ARCADIS, U.S. focusing on infrastructure design. Her specific skills fall within marketing, communication, and information design, as well as graphic and organizational design. She is a member of SMPS Northeast Ohio and is currently serving as the 2013-2014 President. Previous positions include: President-Elect and Membership Chair, Board Member-at-Large, Membership Chair, and a Co-Chair for the Social Committee.

Vanessa served as Researcher/Author for Seller of A/E/C Services Summary of Findings and Analyst/Editor for the Introduction, in addition to compiling author biographies and company information for the book.

Taree Bollinger, CPSM

Taree Bollinger, CPSM, is Vice President of Financial Consulting Solutions Group, which serves the public sector through analysis of cost of service and rate recovery solutions for water, sewer, storm water, electric, solid waste, and transportation infrastructure projects, as well as organizational studies, performance reviews, user fees, and indirect cost allocations for general fund departments. A former SMPS Foundation Trustee, she has authored multiple white papers and articles on A/E/C marketing topics.

Taree served as Researcher/Author for Dependables (Public Sector – State, County, Municipal Government).

Edward A. Bond, Jr., FSMPS, FCMAA, LEED AP

Edward Bond, Jr., FSMPS, FCMAA, LEED AP, is CEO of BOND and has been involved in every facet of the business for over thirty years. BOND is a serial builder for many top clients and Ed has been a trusted advisor and board member of many institutions. He is also a speaker and author of numerous articles.

Ed served as Researcher/Author for Directors (Constructors and Construction Managers).

Janet E. Brooks, CPSM

Janet E. Brooks, CPSM, is Director of Business Development for Clark Nexsen, PC. Her entire career has been within the design and construction industry having worked for both design and construction firms. She has particular expertise in business development, multi-discipline marketing, communications, and public relations.

Janet served as Analyst/Editor for Sharp Shooters (Single-discipline Prime), Entrepreneurs (Corporate, Commercial, Hospitality), and Systems (Educational, Health Care, Institutional).

Emily Crandall, CPSM

Emily Crandall, CPSM, has more than a decade of marketing experience in the design and construction industry. She oversees all corporate marketing initiatives for Horizon Engineering Associates, focusing on internal communications, proposals, and business development strategies.

Emily served as Researcher/Author for Collaborators (Sub-consultants and Specialty Consultants) and Analyst/Editor for Jacks of All Trades (Multi-discipline Design and Planning).

Tracey Gould, MS, IMC

Tracey Gould, M.S., IMC, is the Director of Marketing for Baskervill, a national, award-winning design firm based in Richmond, Virginia. Gould has twenty years of experience in the design and construction industry, has authored multiple articles on marketing and brand strategy, is currently past-president of SMPS Virginia, and serves as an adjust professor in public relations at West Virginia University.

Tracey served as Analyst/Editor for Directors (Constructors and Construction Managers).

Kathryn Hews, CPSM

Kathryn (Katy) Hews, CPSM, Associate Principal for Marketivity, has been in the design and construction industry since the 1970s, with increasing levels of marketing and business development responsibilities for regional, national, and international firms. She has been an active member of SMPS since the mid-1980s, serving as Education Chair for the Denver, Seattle, and Boston chapters. She is a past-president of SMPS Maine.

Katy served as Researcher/Author for Supporters (Not-for-Profits).

Kim Icenhower, FSMPS, CPSM

Kim Icenhower, FSMPS, CPSM, is the President of Icenhower Consulting, LLC, a Marketing, Event, and Campaign Consulting firm in the Houston area. She has more than thirty years of professional services marketing in the design and construction industry.

Kim served as Researcher/Author for Sellers of A/E/C Services Summary and Findings, and Analyst/Editor for Collaborators (Sub-consultants and Specialty Consultants), Jacks of All Trades (Multi-discipline Design and Planning), and Supporters (Not-for-Profits).

Cindy Jackson, FSMPS, CPSM

Cindy Jackson, FSMPS, CPSM, has served as a marketing generalist in the design and construction industry for more than thirty years. Developing relationships, mentoring, and attention to detail are characteristics of this dedicated professional who has been instrumental in marketing successes where she has served as marketing manager, marketing coordinator, and presenter.

Cindy served as Researcher/Author for Systems (Educational, Health Care, Institutional).

Colleen Kucera, CPSM

Colleen Kucera, CPSM, graduated from Arizona State University's, W.P. Carey School of Business, with a Bachelor of Science degree with an emphasis in Marketing. In addition to being a proud mother and wife,

Colleen is the Marketing Manager for Ryan Companies U.S., Inc.'s Southwest Regional Office. Colleen's passion and dedication to the commercial real estate industry extends into her local Arizona Chapter of SMPS where she has served as a Board Member and Past President.

Colleen served as Researcher/Author for Sharp Shooters (Single-discipline Prime) and Jacks of All Trades (Multi-discipline Design and Planning).

Adam Kilbourne, CPSM

Adam Kilbourne, CPSM, is Director of Marketing for Tec Inc. Engineering & Design. He has particular expertise in branding and social media. Adam has authored multiple articles on the topic of social media.

Adam served as Analyst/Editor for Dependables (Public Sector – State, County, Municipal Government) and Supporters (Not-for-Profits), in addition to providing technical support as MySMPS librarian.

Jean Leathers, CPSM

Jean Leathers, CPSM, President of Practice Clarity, LLC, advises A/E/C professionals on building business with new and existing clients. As a nationally recognized consultant with twenty-five years of experience, she helps firms clarify position, create strategy, claim marketplace, and cultivate relationships that lead to work. She is widely published and presents nationally to building design and construction audiences.

Jean served as senior editor and proofreader for the final manuscript.

Melissa Lutz, FSMPS, CPSM

Melissa Lutz, FSMPS, CPSM, is a Principal and the Director of Marketing for Champlin Architecture, a Cincinnati-based architectural and interior design firm focusing on civic, corporate, health care, higher education, and religious projects.

Melissa served as Researcher/Author for Sharp Shooters (Single-discipline Prime).

Nikou McCarra, CPSM

Nikou McCarra, CPSM, is Marketing Director for Shrader Engineering, an electrical and information technology engineering firm. An equal mix of creativity and organizational skill enables Nikou to effectively implement strategic communication tactics for her firm. She specializes in writing, design, and digital marketing.

Nikou served as graphic designer for the book cover.

Lori Miller, CPSM, ExecCoach

Lori Miller, CPSM and Executive Coach, is a senior marketing professional with Perkins Eastman. She provides overall marketing leadership and business development strategies for an international senior living practice across thirteen offices in the United States and abroad.

Lori served as Researcher/Author for Sharp Shooters (Single-discipline Prime).

Dennis Paoletti, FSMPS, FAIA, FASA

Dennis Paoletti, FSMPS, FAIA, FASA, Principal of Paoletti Consulting, has had a prominent forty-five-year career consulting in the areas of architectural acoustics, technology systems, and marketing. He has actively served in a variety of leadership roles in SMPS at local and national levels.

Dennis served as Researcher/Author for Entrepreneurs (Corporate, Commercial, Hospitality).

Craig Park, FSMPS, Assoc. AIA

Craig Park, FSMPS, Assoc. AIA, is a marketing strategist with more than thirty years of experience in the design and construction industry. He is a prolific speaker and writer, and the author of two books on professional practice: The Architecture of Value and The Architecture of Image.

Craig served as Researcher/Author for Systems (Education, Health Care, Institutional).

Mary Beth Perring, FSMPS, CPSM

Mary Beth Perring, FSMPS, CPSM, brings more than twenty-five years of experience leading the marketing efforts for A/E firms, both in-house and as a consultant, to her role of Researcher/Author. A member of SMPS since 1986, and a Fellow since 2003, Mary Beth has been active on a wide variety of committees both at a chapter and national level. Currently a member of the SMPS Indiana chapter, she has provided workshops on a range of marketing topics for SMPS chapters, regional conferences, engineering associations, and university classes, as well as authoring articles for local and national publications.

Mary Beth served as Researcher/Author for Dependables (Public Sector – State, County, Municipal).

Fawn Radmanich, CPSM

Fawn Radmanich, CPSM, is a Senior Marketing Specialist for CDM Smith. She is an on-the-ground proposal developer and pursuit strategist, with particular expertise in public services marketing for multi-million dollar design and construction projects. She specializes in pursuing projects in all areas of water, wastewater, reuse, and design-build.

Fawn served as Analyst/Editor for Dependables (Public Sector – State, County, Municipal) and Systems (Education, Health Care, Institutional).

Cricket Robertson, CPSM

Cricket Robertson, CPSM, is passionate about all things marketing and has been heavily involved in SMPS since moving to Arizona six years ago. She has more than fifteen years of marketing experience having worked for firms in architecture, engineering, and construction. Cricket received her MBA from the University of Phoenix and her BS in International Relations with minors in Business and Russian from Brigham Young University.

Cricket served as Researcher/Author and Analyst/Editor for Directors (Constructors and Construction Managers) and provided proofreading, editing, analysis, and layout for the entire book.

Steve Ryherd, CPSM, LEED AP

Steve Ryherd, CPSM, LEED AP, Principal Consultant with Arpeggio Acoustic Consulting, is a technical professional and Past President of SMPS Atlanta. He holds a Master's degree in Applied Acoustics from Chalmers University of Technology in Gothenburg, Sweden, and a Master's and Bachelor's degree in Architectural Engineering from the University of Nebraska. Steve draws heavily on his experiences in SMPS to enhance the marketing and business development activities of his acoustic consulting business.

Steve served as Researcher/Author for Systems (Education, Health Care, Institutional).

Barbara D. Shuck, FSMPS, CPSM

Barbara Shuck, FSMPS, CPSM, has more than thirty years of experience in marketing, business development, and sales. She is Firm-wide Marketing Communications Manager at Wilson & Company, Inc., Engineers & Architects. She is Secretary/Treasurer on the SMPS National Board, and will be President-Elect in 2013-14. She was SMPS Arizona Chapter President, and received Arizona's Pinnacle Achievement Award in 2004. She served as SMPS National Marketing Communications Awards (MCA) Chair in 2006, and Build Business Conference Chair (Denver) in 2008.

Barbara served as Researcher/Author for Jacks of All Trades (Multi-discipline Design and Planning).

Diana M. Soldano, FSMPS, CPSM

Diana M. Soldano, FSMPS, CPSM, is a seasoned marketing and business development professional in the field of architecture and engineering services. She is currently the Director of Marketing Operations for a multi-disciplinary engineering firm in New York, and is a faculty teacher for business development courses for SMPS.

Diana served as Researcher/Author for Collaborators (Sub-consultants and Specialty Consultants).

Jeffrey Taub, CPSM

Jeffrey Taub, CPSM, is Regional Marketing Manager for the New York and New Jersey offices of VHB. He is a former SMPS New Jersey Chapter President and has authored numerous articles for Real Estate Weekly, Marketer, and industry newsletters on a variety of marketing and business issues.

Jeffrey served as Researcher/Author for Entrepreneurs (Corporate, Commercial, Hospitality).

Katie van der Sleesen

Katie van der Sleesen has held various functions including marketing, operations, quality management, and new business development in large, small, and start-up professional service organizations. She currently serves as Director of Marketing for a national design firm located on the East Coast.

Katie served as Researcher/Author for Directors (Constructors and Construction Managers) and About the SMPS Foundation and SMPS, as well as Analyst/Editor for Sharp Shooters (Single-discipline Prime) and Sellers of A/E/C Services Summary.

Amy Villasana-Moore, CPSM

Amy Villasana-Moore, CPSM, is the Arizona Manager of Marketing & Business Development for Sunrise Engineering, a regional civil engineering and surveying firm. Her career focus has been on the implementation of strategic marketing initiatives that affect changes company-wide.

Amy served as Analyst/Editor for Predictables (Public Sector – Federal Government), and Compiler/Editor for About the SMPS Foundation Thought Leadership Committee.

Joy L. Woo, CPSM, LEED AP

Joy L. Woo, CPSM, LEED AP, has devoted her of more than twenty years to strategic planning, marketing, and operations in a variety roles, including: senior strategic projects manager; global practice, regional, and office marketing director; marketing manager; proposal team leader; and technical editor.

Joy served as Researcher/Author for Entrepreneurs (Corporate, Commercial, Hospitality).

TLS Leadership and Foundation Staff

- Scott W. Braley, FAIA, FRSA—Co-Chair, Foundation Trustee
- Scott D. Butcher, FSMPS, CPSM—Co-Chair, Foundation Trustee
- Donna L. Jakubowicz, FSMPS, CPSM—Foundation President 2011-12
- Dana L. Birkes, FSMPS, CPSM, FPRSA, APR—Foundation President 2012-13
- Lisa S. Bowman—Foundation Staff
- Molly Dall'Erta—Foundation Staff
- Michele D. Santiago, MS—Foundation Staff

Employers of Committee Members

The SMPS Foundation also acknowledges and gives heartfelt thanks the following companies without whose unwavering support the committee members—their employees—could not have put forth this effort. We are most grateful.

- AECOM
- ARCADIS U.S., Inc.
- Arpeggio Acoustic Consulting
- Bartlett Cocke General Contractors
- Barton Malow
- Baskervill
- Bernardin, Lochmueller & Associates
- BKA Architects
- BOND
- Braley Consulting & Training
- CDM Smith
- CHA Architects
- Champlin Architecture
- Clark Nexsen, PC
- Covello Group
- DLR Group
- Emc2 Group Architects Planners
- FCS Group
- Flintco
- Hermosa Construction Group
- Horizon Engineering Associates, LLP
- Icenhower Consulting
- JDB Engineering, Inc.
- KLH Engineers
- Lockwood, Kessler & Bartlett

- Marketivity
- Paoletti Consulting
- Perkins Eastman
- Pfluger Architects
- Practice Clarity
- Ryan Companies US, Inc.
- Shrader Engineering
- Sunrise Engineering, Inc.
- Tec Inc. Engineering & Design
- The Sextant Group
- VHB
- Wilson & Company, Engineers & Architects

15 ABOUT SMPS AND
THE SMPS FOUNDATION

Researcher/Author: Katie van der Sleesen

Analyst/Editor: Scott W. Braley, FAIA, FRSA

The Society for Marketing Professional Services

The Society for Marketing Professional Services' (SMPS) mission is to advocate for, educate, and connect leaders in the building industry. Since its establishment in 1973, SMPS has grown into a network of more than 6,000 marketing and business development professionals from architectural, engineering, planning, interior design, construction, and specialty consulting firms located throughout the United States and Canada. SMPS provides members with networking, business intelligence, research, professional development, leadership opportunities, and marketing resources to help them gain a competitive advantage in positioning their firms successfully in the market place, while advancing their careers. For more information about SMPS, visit www.smps.org, or contact SMPS at (800) 292-7677.

The Society for Marketing Professional Services Foundation

This book is one of many research initiatives funded by the SMPS Foundation. The SMPS Foundation mission is to discover and share what makes architecture/engineering/ construction organizations successful in marketing and business development in an ever-changing marketplace.

The SMPS Foundation is a not-for-profit 501(c)(3) organization established by SMPS to promote research and education that advances the body of knowledge in the field of professional services marketing. For more information on how you can support the Foundation's work, participate in its ongoing research projects, or access past research projects published by the SMPS Foundation, visit www.smpsfoundation.org, or contact SMPS at (800) 292-7677.

16 UNDERWRITERS

Rainmakers
- HDR, Inc.

Door Openers
- Bowie Gridley Architects
- The Brand Constructors
- Scott D. Butcher, FSMPS, CPSM
- Clark Nexsen, PC
- Go! Strategies
- GWWO Inc./Architects
- JDB Engineering, Inc.
- McCarthy Nordburg, Ltd.
- Meyer Najem Construction
- Perkins Eastman
- SMPS Greater Cincinnati
- Wilson & Company, Inc.

Rainmaker Underwriter

HDR is a global employee-owned firm providing architecture, engineering, consulting, construction and related services through our various operating companies. Our professionals are committed to helping clients manage complex projects and make sound decisions. People have access to clean water, sound bridges, hospitals and more, because of the work we do. We wake up every day knowing that our work matters.

Fast Facts

- Founded in 1917

- Headquartered in Omaha, Neb.

- More than 8,000 professionals

- More than 185 locations

- Completed projects in 60 countries

- No. 1 in Modern Healthcare's 2012 "Annual Construction & Design Survey of Healthcare Architects"

- No. 11 in Engineering News-Record's 2012 "Top 500 Design Firms"

Made in the USA
Charleston, SC
02 February 2014

continued to help him up, steady him on his feet, and give him one more day to enjoy a comfy home, love, compassion, and a family.

For you see, we too had made a promise, a promise that we would care for this dog until the end of his days. When the time finally came and our boy left us behind, we stood staring at the homecare vet's tail lights until they became blurry with our tears. We stared and stared until we could no longer see or even hear the vehicle as it crested the hill and passed out of our sight. In the end, it was we who knew the great loss of being left behind, and not Bear Bear, and the irony was not lost on us.

Today we think of him often, and continue to tell the story of the pierced family jewels and giggle as we relate the story. Bear Bear will remain in our hearts until the end of our days and we finally get to hold him again.

৩৫

Melody Whitworth, upon relocating from Florida to Columbia, Missouri, started seeing chained dog after chained dog after chained dog—a concept she could neither accept nor ignore.

Melody is now the President/Director of Unchained Melodies Dog Rescue, whose mission is to rescue, rehabilitate and rehome the chained, penned, abused and neglected back yard dog. Visit unchainedmelodies. org to learn more about this fast growing, all-volunteer organization and how you can support them and their mission.

THE ART OF CLICKER TRAINING COWS
Lefty and Friends

BY RHI BANKS

WHEN WE FINALLY FOUND THE PERFECT PLOT of land on which to build Brother Wolf's Animal Sanctuary, it came with an unexpected challenge: a small herd of undersocialized cows were already calling it their home.

We inquired about what would happen to them if we were to purchase the land, and found that they'd be sent to slaughter. Even then, we understood that the lives of those cows were just as valuable as the lives of the dogs and cats we were working to rescue every day. So when the time came, we negotiated them into our contract to buy the land, and